Praise for This Book

"For once, a book that tells the truth about the expat experience. An inspiring account, and a must-read for those contemplating an international assignment or those already on one."

> —Yvonne McNulty, PhD, Assistant Professor,
> James Cook University, Singapore

"*Expat Women: Confessions* is a wonderful addition to the literature on the experiences of women during their lives abroad. Andrea and Victoria answer difficult questions with empathy, an upbeat attitude, and wisdom. This is a book that every expat woman should keep at her bedside for the moments that inevitably surface when abroad—and even after repatriation."

> —Elizabeth Perelstein, President, School Choice
> International, and named one of Fortune Magazine's
> 10 Most Powerful Women Entrepreneurs (2010)

"With the voice of your most resourceful girlfriends, Andrea and Victoria give expat women worldwide a fabulous collection of practical advice."

> —Kathleen Simon, President, and My-Linh Kunst, 1st
> Vice President Communications, FAWCO (Federation
> of American Women's Clubs Overseas Inc.)

"Expatriation can be very rewarding and yet a challenge at the same time, but it is, for everyone, a life-changing experience. This is a comprehensive book about diverse expat experiences and I believe it could be a useful point of reference for those seeking encouragement and understanding in meeting the challenges they face. It made me realize how fortunate we are to work in a company that invests in expatriate support."

> —Karin Brakel, Global Outpost Manager, Shell International B.V.

Praise for This Book

. . . .

"An inspiring book which gives a great insight into expatriate life."

> —Elske van Holk, Director, Expatriate Archive Centre,
> The Netherlands

"Living abroad can be a mind-opening experience that enhances your personal and professional lives, but it can also be a lonely place. *Expat Women: Confessions* eases that loneliness by collecting many of the challenges faced by expats and offering practical solutions to problems unique to the globetrotting woman."

> —Stacie Nevadomski Berdan, Co-author, *Get Ahead by Going Abroad: A Woman's Guide to Fast-track Career Success*, and Author, *Go Global! A Student's Guide to Launching an International Career*

"A very interesting, easy-to-read and helpful companion guide for women trailing their spouses around the world."

> —Missy Dover, Director of Global Mobility,
> The McGraw-Hill Companies

"With regard to all matters of mobility, knowledge adds a powerful tool: for the assignment manager, for service partners, and perhaps most importantly, for expats and their families. We can always applaud work that adds clarity to the international assignment process."

> —Peggy Smith, SCRP, SGMS, CEO, Worldwide ERC®

Expat Women: Confessions

50 Answers to Your Real-Life Questions about Living Abroad

Andrea Martins & Victoria Hepworth

Published by Expat Women Enterprises Pty Ltd ATF Expat Women Trust, PO Box 518, Cotton Tree, QLD, 4558, Australia, www.expatwomen.com

Copyedited by Naomi Pauls, Paper Trail Publishing
Cover design by Beth Nori, Nori Studios
Internal design by Melissa Gerber, Melissa Gerber Graphic Design
Printed by Lightning Source
Images by Shutterstock

ISBN 978-0-9808236-0-8

10 9 8 7 6 5 4 3 2 1

Disclaimer: All of the confessions in this book are based on real-life experiences of real-life expatriate women living abroad. Some confessions were based on submissions to ExpatWomen.com and some were based on the authors' general observations abroad. This is a general interest book that aims to provide useful information and ideas to women living, or thinking of living, abroad. This book is not comprehensive and does not claim to offer professional advice of any kind. Readers of this book are responsible for consulting their own competent professional advisors for personal, legal, financial or other counsel tailored to their individual circumstances. ExpatWomen.com, the authors, editors, contributors, publishers, sponsors, designers, distributors and promoters will not be held accountable for any errors, omissions or damages arising from information contained in this book.

To all of the wonderful expatriate women across the globe. There are fun times and there are tough times, but at all times, believe in yourself and know that you are not alone.

Contents

Foreword by Robin Pascoe 17

Introduction by Andrea Martins 21

Chapter 1: Settling In 25
Transitioning Quickly 26
Why Should I Move? 29
Will Culture Shock Happen to Me? 34
Becoming a Trailing Spouse 37
I Am a Citizen, but I Cannot Settle In 40
Starting Your Own Club 43
Beware of Your Friends 47
Feeling Unwelcome 51
Household Help 55

Chapter 2: Career and Money 59
Loss of Career 60
My Job Was a Mistake 63
Work-Life Balance 67
Lack of Respect at Work 71
I Need More Than Coffee 75
Starting a Business 79

Confused About Finances 84
Show Me the Money 89
No Money Left 93

Chapter 3: Raising Children 99

Pregnant, Far from Home 100
Homesick New Mother Abroad 104
International Adoption 108
Raising Bilingual Children 114
Special Needs Children 119
My Teenagers Are Not Adapting 123
Teen Suicide 128
My Kids Are My All 133
Empty Nest 137

Chapter 4: Relationships 141

My Trailing Man 142
Intercultural Couple 146
He Wants to Go Home 150
Keeping Secrets 153
Divorce Abroad 157
Picking Up the Pieces 161
Domestic Violence 165
Expat Infidelity 170
Online Betrayal 175
A Lonely Affair 179

Chapter 5: Mixed Emotions 183

Overcoming Negativity 184
Medical Treatment Abroad 187
Holiday Sadness 192
I Think I Am an Alcoholic 195
Adult TCK 198

Friends Back Home 202

Retiring Abroad 205

Aging Parents 210

Chapter 6: Repatriation 215

Sudden Exit 216

Death Abroad 219

Visa Expiry 224

An Affair Upon Repatriation 228

Reverse Culture Shock 232

Conclusion 237

Acknowledgments 239

About the Authors 241

About ExpatWomen.com 245

ExpatWomen.com Testimonials 246

Resources 249

Foreword

First, a confession of my own: I have been a longtime fan of the Expat Confessions column on ExpatWomen.com—the extremely readable and appropriately named website that Andrea Martins co-created and works tirelessly to maintain. Both Andrea and Victoria Hepworth, a trained psychologist, should be congratulated for their tremendous service to the far-flung community of expatriate women living abroad, first with their monthly Expat Confessions column and now with this wonderful volume in print.

Second confession: when Andrea asked me to write this foreword, I was not sure "confession" was the right word to include in the book's title. To me, the meaning of "confession" was more in keeping with the one in my desk-side dictionary: "an acknowledgement of one's faults or crimes." Since when, I wondered, did it become a crime to be an expat woman? Then, of course, it hit me. Many women *feel* they are somehow letting the side down by not knowing everything there is to know about living and loving globally. Too often they also feel they are the *only* ones worrying or wondering, so to publicly, albeit anonymously, pose their question really is akin to making a confession.

Depending on where you are posted and what your particular

circumstances are, remaining silent about your concerns can be a survival tactic. Consequently, many expats simply do not want to question or speak up about the challenges of international relocation, so they just slap a smile on their face that may remain frozen there for years! After more than two decades of writing for and lecturing to expat families around the world (and learning too many secrets to count), I am still surprised at the number of women who are afraid to appear anything less than perfectly well adjusted.

But life is too short and the overseas opportunities for cultural experiences, new friendships and personal transformation so numerous that women need to know they are not alone in experiencing a bad day or even wanting to run back "home." Everyone handles transition differently. As many of us in the culture shock "business" like to say, there is no right or wrong, only different. But I still worry, even after all these years of meeting expats, that when women go into denial about challenges, and literally repress these issues for years, this cannot possibly be good for their physical or emotional health. Better to get everything out into the open to enable us to move on and take advantage of the considerable privileges of living abroad.

In *Expat Women: Confessions—50 Answers to Your Real-Life Questions about Living Abroad*, women are encouraged to air their issues, learn that others often feel exactly the same way, and find comfort, reassurance and, often, validation in the knowledge that their own feelings are real and not imagined. Thankfully, the authors have not shied away from addressing tough questions about the "hidden" aspects of global living, such as domestic violence, infidelity and alcohol abuse. These are issues that few people want to acknowledge exist, despite all the evidence to the contrary.

Another message in this book is the importance of supporting one another abroad. I have been incredibly lucky to have both authors step up to be my own extremely supportive expatriate girlfriends.

Andrea is now in Kuala Lumpur, but she and I met when her family was posted to Mexico City. We were communicating about website matters when I finally asked: "By the way, where in the world are you?" When she said Mexico, I seized the chance to say I had always wanted to lecture there. The next thing I knew, I was busy speaking at various locations around Mexico City, including speaking to the Newcomers Club of Mexico City in Andrea's own living room.

Likewise, I met Victoria, who is in Dubai at the moment, in Shanghai when Lifeline Shanghai (a hotline for the city's international community, which she founded) was coincidentally celebrating its first anniversary around the time I was planning to visit. Again, within days, Victoria had my entire program organized.

Many are the adventures and laughs I shared with both women. I hope that when they embark on their own book tours, they too will find new expat girlfriends who offer them the support and friendship they so kindly extended to me.

If there is one message contained within these fifty confessions and the thoughtful responses to each of them, it is this: the challenges of expat women are universal. While locations, languages, weather and food may change, when expat women support one another, as Andrea and Victoria do so well in the pages to follow, it will *always* make a difference.

Enjoy your time abroad, and *keep supporting one another,*

Robin Pascoe

—Director, ExpatExpert.com, and author of *A Broad Abroad: The Expat Wife's Guide to Successful Living Abroad; Raising Global Nomads: Parenting Abroad in an On-Demand World; A Moveable Marriage: Relocate Your Relationship Without Breaking It;* and *Homeward Bound: A Spouse's Guide to Repatriation.*

Introduction

April Davidson was twenty-three and had never left the United States. In mid-2005, April's world was turned upside down. She moved to Mexico City, where her husband's company had sent him to help with local operations. April arrived with two young children in tow, little Spanish, and none of the established expat support infrastructure enjoyed by employee families of larger, multinational companies.

Four months after arriving, April called me to inquire about the playgroup at my house that afternoon. My name and number were listed with the Newcomers Club of Mexico City, and I would often get phone calls from new arrivals and long-termers alike.

"Hi, my name is April... Is this Andrea?" she inquired tentatively.

"Hi, April. Yes, this is Andrea. How can I help you?" I replied, juggling my attention between April and my one-year-old daughter making a mess of the cheese tortillas at the kitchen table.

"I'm calling to ask if you have a playgroup today. I got your number from the Newcomers Club and was wondering if my children and I could come along?" April asked, sounding more confident.

"Yes, four o'clock," I replied. "How old are your children?"

"Madison is three and Tommy is one and a half," April answered.

"Perfect. Please come along at four o'clock. We usually get anywhere from twenty to sixty people, including children. Everyone is really fabulous, and I am sure they would love to meet you."

By the way, "How long have you been in Mexico, April?"

"We've been here four months," she answered. "But I do not speak much Spanish, so the children and I haven't really been out of the apartment yet. Except to buy groceries, of course."

Oh, my, gosh! I thought to myself. *How could she have been here four months and hardly ventured out of the apartment?* I am no superwoman, but by the time I had been in Mexico City for four months, I had explored nearly every inch of my neighborhood, walked my son in his stroller twice a day around the nearby park inhabited by questionable armed guards, been swindled by many of the local food stalls, embarrassed myself speaking Spanish, suffered a few dubious leg waxes at the local salons, attended several Newcomers Club gatherings, and learned how to drive on the opposite side of the road. Sure, I had shed some tears along the way, but more importantly, I had overcome my fears and met some fantastic expat mentors who were invaluable during my settling-in period.

April's experience got me thinking. *Why had our experiences been so different? Was it because I had lived abroad before that I knew a little better how to "jump in"? Did being ten years older help boost my confidence? What was it?*

Fast-forward one year, to mid-2006. April and I had become friends and visited each other often for children's play dates. Fellow expat Jill Lengré and I were working hard behind the scenes to get ExpatWomen.com ready to launch the following January. I asked April if she would please read Robin Pascoe's book *A Moveable Marriage: Relocate Your Relationship without Breaking It* and write a review for our soon-to-be-launched website. April happily volunteered to read Robin's excellent "common sense advice" book.

But never did I anticipate what happened next.

April returned Robin's book to me the following week with tears in her eyes. She took a deep breath as she plucked up the courage to confess: "I never knew that anyone else felt this way. I thought it was just me who felt alone and unable to cope well. I have been taking medication for unexplained stomach problems since arriving, and now my doctor has me on medication for anxiety as well—to help me sleep at night. Finally I understand what is happening. I'm so happy to know that it's not just me."

I stood in my doorway, shocked. April might have taken a while to settle in, but she was always so happy on the outside. I had never imagined she might still be secretly struggling and have something to confess on the inside.

"Do you have any more of Robin's books?" April quipped with a smile, trying to lighten the mood.

Interestingly, April was no novice at relocation: she had relocated domestically ten times before graduating from high school. So what was it about relocating abroad that had overwhelmed her? How can we reassure women that they are *not alone* and provide some more "common sense advice" to help?

It is questions like these that inspired ExpatWomen.com's Expat Confessions column, and it is April and emails from hundreds of women like her who have inspired this book.

My co-author Victoria Hepworth and I thank you very much for supporting this book. We hope that it encourages and inspires you.

Wishing you success abroad,

Andrea Martins

—Director and co-founder, ExpatWomen.com

Chapter 1

Settling In

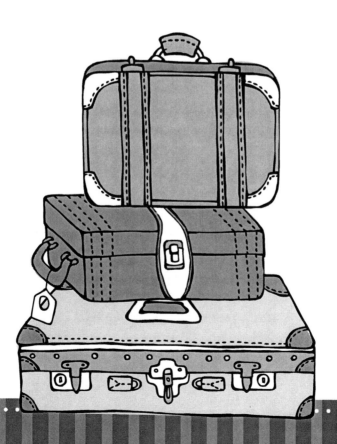

Transitioning Quickly

Q. I am moving to my first overseas posting with my company in two months' time. From what I have heard it can be quite difficult to settle in, and culture shock can cause some problems. I am relocating to Europe on my own and will be starting my new job immediately. Do you have any tips on adjusting to my new life so I can settle in quickly and hopefully avoid any nasty culture shock?

A. Congratulations on the new job! You have heard correctly about the "difficulties" some expatriates face when on the move. Unfortunately there is no way to protect yourself one hundred percent from these feelings and experiences. However, being aware that culture shock exists and that your host country and its people are different from you goes a long way in helping to prevent some of the very real symptoms of culture shock. Many an expatriate has gone abroad unprepared and expected their new locale to be the same as their home country. Needless to say, they have been heavily disappointed when, for example, they discover that people live in apartments rather than houses, late night supermarket shopping is a dream of the future, and, depending on their location, English may not be written or spoken anywhere!

Get to know your new location in advance. Research, research and research some more. Shock comes more to those who are not prepared. So spend as much time as possible researching your new home location and office environment. Go online and learn as much as you can about both the country and its people. If you can travel to your new location for a "look-see visit," go. To help orient you in your new location, if your company offers the service of a friendly destination service consultancy, even better.

Seek out the expatriate clubs, business associations, sporting groups or other social clubs that interest you. These groups are both a vital lifeline for newcomers and an excellent local source of information. Make contact with these clubs before you leave home and ask to be included on their mailing list. Making contact now helps in two ways. First, you may have questions about what to bring, about visa issues or about housing, and the administrator or members of these clubs may be able to answer your questions— or at least point you in the right direction. Second, making contact now ensures that when you arrive in your new home, you will not be all alone. Pre-arrival contact can also ease nerves when showing up to your first social gathering abroad.

If possible, RSVP to a business meeting, luncheon or coffee morning before you even get on the plane, so you have something in your calendar and a commitment to someone in your new location. The longer you leave it to get out and explore your new community, the more difficult it becomes and the harder it is to muster up the courage. Actively making inroads into unfamiliar territory can give you that sense of control you may suddenly feel like you have lost. And there is nothing more comforting than meeting a kindred spirit in your first few weeks in a new place. Most people love to be the "expert" in a situation and offer advice. Capitalize on this generosity and ask as many questions as possible.

Learn the local language. If you do not speak the language of your new location, learn at least the basics before you arrive. This will help you better understand and enjoy your new home, as well as lessen the impact of culture shock on arrival.

Try to leave judgments behind. Once you have landed and become acquainted with the lay of the land, try your very hardest not to compare your new location to your old location. As frustrating or surprising as things might be in your new home, comparing it to your previous location will only hinder your ability to settle in. If you accept that different people and cultures have different ways of operating, this should also help reduce nasty culture shock symptoms.

Be realistic. While these tips may help to reduce the impact of culture shock, they will not eliminate it completely. When researching your host country and preparing yourself for life there, expect that you *will* experience some frustration and uneasiness settling into a new culture—that is only natural. Make sure you give yourself some time to adjust to all the newness and go easy on yourself. Find some mentors in your new location and befriend some expat life coaches if you can, as these contacts will help you form a support network that will become invaluable over time.

And remember, despite the potential culture shock and all the uneasiness that goes with unfamiliar territory, try to smile. You are about to embark on an incredible journey and hopefully have an experience of a lifetime!

Why Should I Move?

Q. My husband has just been offered a one-year assignment in Ireland and I am thinking about whether or not to quit my job and move away from my ill mother to join him. I have no aspirations to live abroad, I am really very content and happy with my life here, and I feel duty bound to be here for my mother. I have thought about living apart from my husband: I understand it would be difficult, but it is an option I am considering, even though I know this would not be the best scenario for our new marriage. All I can think about are the things that I would be giving up and losing out on if I moved. Could you please give me some idea of the positives attached to living the expat life, to convince me to give it a go?

A. For some people it is a real struggle to give up (or take leave from) their work and current identity to follow their partner's career overseas—leaving behind family, friends and everything that is familiar. For others it feels like a real blessing to be handed an escape ticket for a while—an amazing chance to be adventurous and try a new life.

Endless possibilities. However you choose to look at it, one of the major benefits of moving abroad as a trailing spouse (or an "accompanying partner") is the freedom to have your very own blank canvas. You can use the time to do what you have always wanted to do: take time to simply relax, get out and explore your new city, travel in and around your new country, meet new people, start your own business, further your education, get healthy, pursue a new or favorite hobby, take cultural classes, learn a new language, "give back" via local charity organizations, spend some quality time with your partner and/or children without as many time pressures as before, dabble in the stock market, regularly enjoy your newspaper and a latte in a corner café, and more. The possibilities are endless if you choose to find them and make the most of your "time out."

Financial benefits. For many expats, one of the attractions in accepting an overseas assignment is the potential financial benefit. A traditional employer-sponsored expatriate package tends to include accommodation, health insurance, children's education costs, home utilities, flights home, as well as additional incentives that can sometimes make the choice to go abroad quite convincing.

Be warned though: expat packages are like airline tickets—negotiate the deal that is right for you, but then never ask your neighbor what they (are) paid, as it is sure to be different to what you (are) paid. Also, many a well-paid expat has returned home without much to show for it, so be smart with your money and consult a financial advisor if necessary.

The chance to travel. Being abroad typically puts you closer to a whole range of new, different and exciting locations to explore—places that might not have been so easy for you to travel to before. This is a wonderful opportunity to see more of the world, and most seasoned expatriates exploit this new proximity at every public holiday and annual leave opportunity.

Cultural and social enrichment. Your new life abroad will give you the chance to meet many people—both expats and locals. Social clubs and local associations offer an excellent forum for meeting others and can provide you with a rewarding support network in the absence of family and friends back home. Generally the expat community is very warm, supportive and friendly, so it is easy to meet people and form friendships. Furthermore, close friendships in the expat world often form very quickly as you share the frustrations, excitement, fears and challenges of living in the unfamiliar. And if you do not find a group, network or association that interests you, do not be afraid to set one up yourself. (See *Starting Your Own Club*)

Tips for leaving family. Leaving family members is one of the most common concerns facing the ever-growing population of expatriates. Whatever your age, background or cultural identity, leaving family, particularly if they are ill or aging, is never easy. Here are some tips we have collected from expats along the way, which we hope you find helpful and relevant to your situation. (See also *Aging Parents*)

✻ Make sure your company knows your family situation and negotiate into your contract flight tickets home, and possibly extra leave for the working partner.

✻ Call your mother at least once every week, at about the same time if possible.

✻ Plan to go home as often as you realistically can and make sure your mother is aware of these plans. Your visits will give her something to look forward to.

✻ In confidence, try to speak to your mother's bank manager, health provider, gardener, insurance broker, and so on. Make sure they understand that your mother is aging, ill, forgetful or alone, and ask them to help maintain your mother's affairs accordingly. Ask her doctor to call her and make frequent, scheduled appointments.

✻ Make sure you have a "permission to inquire" or "power of attorney" form signed and lodged with her doctor and all other necessary agencies, so they can talk to you freely without breaching privacy or confidentiality regulations.

✻ Ask a close relative or familiar neighbor whether they could look in on your mother on a regular basis, specifically to make sure there is food in the cupboard, the phone and electricity are working and your mother seems okay.

* If your mother needs it, arrange for Meals on Wheels or another non-profit organization that cares for the weak to regularly call in on your mother, especially during the winter months.

* Try to get your mother into a group of some sort—bridge club, church choir, book group—to keep her occupied and surrounded by friends and people she can trust and whom you can contact if you need to.

* Make sure you have the contact numbers of neighbors, relatives and friends, in case you need to call them. It is also a good idea to give them your contact information.

* If your mother is able to use email and possibly the Internet, encourage her to do so—teach her and support her if necessary— so she can feel more connected to you and her friends if she is not seeing everyone as often.

* Consider putting extra credit onto her phone bill, so she can feel free to call you abroad whenever necessary, without fear of the cost of the phone call(s).

The verdict. As with most things, there is a list of positives and negatives applicable to living abroad. Living abroad is not always easy, but nine times out of ten, it brings rich rewards and adds a new dimension to your life that you will most likely treasure in the years to come.

Having said that, if you feel you are genuinely in a situation where your mother needs your care and attention, then perhaps no amount of money, travel or socializing abroad could compare to the value of quality time you are able to devote to your mother at home. Weigh the pros and cons, consider your mother's specific condition, and also bear in mind your new marriage—is it strong enough to survive time apart or time abroad if it is against your will? If you do decide to "give it a go" and accompany your husband but find living abroad unbearable, can you always go home?

These are questions that only you can answer and we wish you all the best with your decision-making.

Will Culture Shock Happen to Me?

Q. Greetings from Vancouver, Canada. My husband and I are on the verge of our first expatriate assignment and are very excited to be moving to London. I think that this will be a very easy transition for us, as English is our first language and the English way of life and culture seems rather similar to our own.

However, an experienced expat friend warned me that sometimes it is more difficult to settle into English-speaking countries as opposed to countries where residents speak another language and have a completely different culture. How could settling into a similar country be more difficult than moving to a country that is vastly different? Surely this was just her personal experience and not typical of expats on the whole, right?

A. Congratulations on your impending move abroad. This is a very exciting time for you and hopefully the start of a chapter in your lives that you will remember and cherish forever.

It is completely possible that your friend had a tougher time adjusting to an English-speaking location than she may have had in the past transitioning into a non-English-speaking location. There are many factors that determine whether someone settles into a location well, just as there are many different expatriates out there with many diverse experiences to share.

Personality and attitude. A positive and open attitude right from the very beginning, a willingness to move abroad, and a good understanding of the location you will be moving to will all help to make an expatriate posting successful, regardless of a location's cultural and linguistic similarities or differences to your home base.

Managing expectations. Expectations also play an important role in a successful assignment abroad. For example, you would expect that moving to a central African country might be a difficult transition because as a Canadian, you are most likely different in the way you look, the language you speak, the food you eat and the values you adhere to. You expect living in central Africa to be difficult, exciting, scary and frustrating, and you prepare yourself and your family accordingly—giving yourself ample time to adjust. In contrast, when English-speaking expats move to an English-speaking country, they typically expect life to be mostly the same and only allow minimal time to adjust. They are often not prepared for the myriad of emotions that comes with relocating—leaving everyone and everything familiar; moving house and belongings; dealing with potentially resentful children, and so on.

Companies tend to think the same. They expect a move to an "easy" country to go smoothly and usually put more emphasis on providing support (such as cross-cultural training, language lessons, an internal buddy system, help with accommodation, and so on) for transitions to "difficult" locations instead.

The local community's expectations may also impact whether an expatriate settles in quickly and with ease. In a country where you are obviously foreign, you may be excused for any cultural faux pas and what may be viewed as cultural ignorance. This may not be the case in a community where you look the same and thus expectations of you are the same as for the local community.

Support networks. In non-English-speaking locations, the expat community usually bands together and opportunities to meet people are readily available (via expat associations, business networks and various activity-specific groups). Newsletters, websites and local expat magazines publicize information about these events, and it is relatively easy to find a club and/or an event that interests you to attend. Expatriates tend to look out for one another and the community tends to be supportive and close-knit.

However, English-speaking countries do not always have the same established support networks for foreigners—perhaps because there is an expectation that in an English-speaking country, expatriate English speakers can go and join any group they please. Facilities that expats may require, such as religious services, sports clubs, business networks, child care and the general opportunity to meet people are usually already available in the local community for anybody to use.

Yet the local patrons of these community facilities usually already have their network of friends and are less likely to feel the need to reach out and meet new people—especially newcomers who are likely to be transient. So, as a newcomer in an English-speaking country, you need to make a concerted effort to socialize, get to know people and get them to know you. This is not impossible, it just involves a little more work, and you do need to shape your expectations accordingly.

Work prospects. Another factor not often considered is the potential difficulty for an accompanying partner to work in an English-speaking location. While sometimes work opportunities may be easier to find, other times candidate competition may be fiercer because English-speaking skills are not considered as precious a commodity as in a non-English-speaking locale.

So, your friend was right: sometimes it is more difficult to settle into English-speaking countries. However, managing your expectations through research and investing a little extra effort to make contacts when you arrive will give you the best possible start to your time abroad. Enjoy yourself!

Becoming a Trailing Spouse

Q. I was previously employed at home and now find myself at a loss as a trailing spouse in Saint Petersburg, Russia. I do not speak Russian and even if I could find a job, legally it is not possible for me to work here. Suddenly the days are very long, I have difficulty filling them and am starting to dread going to bed because it means I wake up with another day to face. I have never experienced this before and feel so useless. The small wonders that I do manage to achieve (like finally getting wireless set up) take all my energy and leave me questioning my ability to do anything at all. Any tips on how I can turn my experience here into a positive one?

A. The transition from life as an independent, busy and successful executive to a nonworking spouse can take its toll on anyone. Throw in the stresses of a foreign country, local bureaucracy and a new language, and you really do have a lot to adjust to.

You are not alone. It is important for you to know that you are not alone in your frustration as a trailing spouse (or "accompanying partner") abroad. The demographic profile of the typical expatriate has been changing: no longer are expat postings reserved for the most senior managers. Overseas assignments are also increasingly essential for lower- and middle-management employees who want to further their career and impress their superiors. This means that in addition to the senior managers, many expat couples abroad are now young, educated and concerned with their dual careers.

As a group, the trailing spouses of today are also different. There are more male trailing spouses (although the majority are still women), and the female trailing spouses are having children later—allowing them more time at this point in their lives to pursue (and be more vocal about) their own career agenda. Generally speaking, many more options are available to women these days, as to what they can expect to achieve with their lives and their careers, and this is affecting expectations when women live abroad.

Ask for assistance. Some companies offer trailing spouses assistance in their transition. This assistance could be access to an expat life coach, useful books or web resources to address some of your concerns. You could get access to a career counselor, with whom you could discuss alternative career options, which might enable you to continue adding skills to your résumé via nontraditional employment. Or you could be given introductions to local networks that might interest you. Talk to your partner's Human Resources department and see whether they could offer any assistance to help you kick-start your new life abroad.

Stick to a schedule. In terms of helping day to day, do you have a daily routine? A regular schedule can help you look forward to and keep you accountable to achieve certain things each day. At a time when you feel that everything is up in the air, a routine can be a savior.

For example, set your alarm or get up when your partner gets up, so you do not stay in bed all day. The opportunity to sleep late each day may seem like a luxury, but when you believe you have nothing to get up for you are on a slippery slope into depression. Set yourself a morning routine, whether eating breakfast and reading the newspaper, responding to emails for an hour, doing the laundry, grocery shopping or something else. Plan what time you will shower, how long you will read the newspaper, where you will take that walk, which new lunch place you will try, which tourist site you will visit each week, and so on.

Make a daily to-do list, so that at the end of the day you can see what you have achieved. Checking off items on that list can help you feel good about yourself and a bit more in control each day. The better you feel about yourself, the more control you feel you have over a situation. And with control, more often than not, the happier you are with your partner and your new location, and the more open you usually are to new opportunities—such as new friendships, employment, travel, new projects and more.

Get active and be creative. Exercise is another liberator. It makes you feel better about yourself, gets you out of the house, and it makes you feel you have been productive. Exercise is also known to counter depression and feelings of sadness, so if you are feeling low, try to incorporate exercise into your daily schedule so you can benefit from some of those feel-good endorphins.

As for the big picture, we encourage you to be creative in your thinking about how to spend your days. Get involved in expat clubs, professional associations or groups that interest you. Start your own club (see *Start Your Own Club*). Volunteer. Learn the local language. Study—locally, online or via correspondence. Explore your city. Think about what you might be able to do if you worked virtually— based at home but working for a company based outside of your current country. Document your experiences in a journal or online via a blog. Write a book. Plan your next vacation. Think about starting your own business—either now, if local laws permit, or for where you move to next. (See *Starting a Business*)

Incredible opportunity. There are many possible projects out there for intelligent women like you. With each new day, you have a blank canvas at your fingertips. This can be daunting but is also an incredible opportunity, once you start to think of it that way.

Good luck with your transition.

I Am a Citizen, but I Cannot Settle In

Q. I was born in Asia and went to London at age twenty-five. I studied, worked, lived and met my American husband in London. Well, it has been fourteen years since we married, and we have lived in different countries in Asia for the past ten years.

Most times, I have found meaningful and gainful employment abroad to insulate myself from the frustrations of feeling "lost" in each new location. However, we recently relocated to the United States, and with neither a job offer nor any experience living in the U.S. before, I am having difficulties fitting into the country of my current passport. I am forty now—and I am afraid that I am no longer as gung-ho as I was when I first started my free-spirited life—so I have not ventured far yet from our house in suburbia. Do you have any ideas about how to integrate with other foreign-born Americans—and find meaning for my new life in the United States?

A. It sounds like you have a few different concerns: you feel isolated from others in your community; you feel anxious to face your new environment; and you are searching for something meaningful to achieve in your new home country. Let us look at these one by one.

Overcoming isolation. As a seasoned expat, you are probably acutely aware of that feeling of isolation that new expats generally experience. It may not take on the same shape or form in each country, which makes it even more difficult to deal with, but it is there and common all the same. I guess you never would have expected to feel so alone in a country of which you are a citizen, especially since you seem to have lived successfully abroad for many years.

Believe it or not, it is often more difficult to meet people in a developed society or community than it is in other places. Just because you are an American citizen does not mean you do not have to work at meeting people—you probably have to work harder. Have you taken the same steps to integrate in the United States as you did in previous postings, such as researching local associations, clubs and networks? Many times, there are groups out there, if you just remember to look for them. Once you immerse yourself into the community and meet some people, your confidence will increase and daily living will not be so intimidating. Friends and acquaintances are important in creating a sense of belonging to a community.

Experiencing culture shock. Or could it be that you are struggling with the sudden shift from "exotic Asia" to the slower life of suburbia? For many people, this would be called "reverse culture shock" (see *Reverse Culture Shock*), but if you have never lived in suburban America before, for you it would be simply called "culture shock."

Perhaps it would help if you recalibrated your mindset so that you *did* think your location was exciting and bursting with things for you to do—just as you probably thought when you were overseas. Look around as a tourist in your own area and do the things tourists (or indeed, new expats) would do. Make an effort to make your new American life exciting!

Taking it one step at a time. Unless there is a tangible fundamental explanation for your reluctance to go out of your neighborhood, there is nothing to wait for. Go for it! Set yourself attainable goals each day: walk to the end of the street and back, buy a newspaper each day, take a book and have morning coffee at the local café, visit the local library, go and get your hair cut—as hairdressers are always up for a conversation and can usually give you some gossip about what is going on around town. Such small steps will gradually increase your confidence to do more.

Communicating. Have you explained your feelings to your husband? Ask him for support and plan to take a trip into town together this weekend. Make a restaurant reservation and have dinner together in your local area. Small steps like this should help you become familiar with your surroundings and feel more and more comfortable about living in them. Maybe you do not have the same gung-ho attitude you had when you first moved to the United Kingdom, but step back and reevaluate who you are now and what you want to get out of your life now as an experienced woman, traveler and expat. Perhaps you are trying to be the same person you once were and putting unnecessary pressure on yourself to live the free-spirited life?

Finding meaning. Which brings us to the final point: finding some meaning in this chapter of your life. Make a list of the things that are important to you, the things you would dearly love to achieve and ways you might go about achieving them. Then sign up with the clubs or associations in your area that match your list of priorities. Trust your instincts. Follow your passions—these might just be the magnets that you need to attract new friends and supporters into this new chapter of your life.

Starting a club. Finally, if you do not meet the foreign-born Americans you were hoping to meet, you can always start a new club to attract them (see *Starting Your Own Club*). After all, there are sure to be other foreign-born Americans in your area who would love the opportunity to get together, just like you. With a bit of research, some small steps and a little soul-searching, we are confident you can soon feel at home in the United States, just like you did elsewhere.

Best wishes.

Starting Your Own Club

Q. Hi there. We are living in a very small village in Finland. We have been here for seven months now and I am still having a hard time meeting people. I know there are foreigners living here, but there seem to be no expat clubs or associations that bring us together. I have joined some online forums, but it is not quite the same as meeting someone for a coffee. What can I do?

A. Have you thought about starting your own club? Sometimes expat life calls for improvisation and resourcefulness. This is a perfect example of such a time. You feel your community is lacking in clubs for the foreign population, so why not set one up yourself?

You can bet that if you are feeling this lack, others in your community are feeling it too. Speaking from experience, establishing your own club can be a lot of fun, plus a great way to get to know people and get out there in the community. In addition to benefiting future members, such a club can also become a valuable project in which to invest your energy (especially if you are unable to work) and something you can put on your résumé.

Here are some pointers to consider when starting your own club. Feel free to pick and choose which ideas to pursue.

Consider the type of members. Think about what type of people you would like to meet. Other professional women? Mothers and toddlers? A certain nationality? Any foreigner in your community? Expats with an interest in a specific sport, hobby or leisure activity?

Think about the type of organization. After thinking about possible members, decide what type of organization you would like to have and what it will provide for its members. Will your new club have a professional focus, with monthly speakers on work-related issues? Or will it be a group that shares general information in a casual environment? Will it be purely a social group? Will the group have an articulated mission? Will each meeting have a structured agenda? How can new people join the group and what is the benefit of becoming a group member?

Choose a name for the group. International Women's Club of Finland? Professional Women's Group of Finland? Friends of Finland? Make sure the name you choose is appropriate, captures the "essence" of your club and does not duplicate the name of another group. Remember to check whether other associations elsewhere have the same name or aim as your group. You might be able to align your two groups, and even if they are not located in the same area, you might still be able to provide support to each other.

Decide where and when you will hold meetings. Will you find a coffeehouse or hotel meeting room and arrange to meet there the same time each month? Or will you meet at someone's house? Will you meet each week, each month, or every time a certain sports team plays?

Go online and set up an email address. Gmail, Hotmail, Yahoo! and similar free providers make good web hosts. They are also very convenient if you have others who will help you check club emails from different physical locations. Ideally, set up the email address in the club's name, so that if you move on, the email address is not attached to your personal name.

Email anyone and everyone. Send a welcome message to all those you have met in your host country who you feel might be interested or know of someone who could be interested, and ask them if they would like to join your group's mailing list. Sometimes a short list of email addresses can grow exponentially in record time.

People are often waiting for active people like you to do the work and get things moving. As they say, "Build it and they will come."

Market your club. You may want to approach relevant local organizations whose members might be interested in your new club, such as chambers of commerce, schools, gyms, companies that host expatriates where you live, and so on. Although probably not in your local village, you might also like to inform any embassies or consulates in your region, as they might field inquiries from people who do live in your village.

Set up a website or blog. Setting up a website or blog these days is relatively easy. Perhaps begin with a blog—which is like an online diary—because it is very easy to start and update. Then if you find someone in your group who can help set up a website, you can always migrate your information to a website, or keep both the blog and website active—to increase the chances of a newcomer finding you on the Web.

List your website or blog on expat directories. Once you have a web presence, tell people about it. Get your website or blog listed on relevant expatriate sites and local sites for your village.

Find board members. Give your new club a few months to see how people react and what response you get. If you feel the club is successful, you may want to form a board and thus get a few other people involved to help you run the club.

Get official. Eventually you may want and/or need to develop a constitution and register your organization with the necessary authorities, especially if you choose to take membership money from members. These official measures might not be needed at the beginning, but bear in mind that you may need to consider them down the track, depending on what type of club you decide to run and its activities.

Remember your members. One of the perks of starting your own club is that you are in charge and can take it as far as your inclination, energy and willingness allow. You can also change the direction of the club after you start it. However, if your club grows big or changes direction, do try to remember why your members joined in the first place and how best to gain their support as you move forward.

Give it a go. So, why not start your own club? Even if your club does not survive long term, this is a great short-term opportunity for you to meet more people and for more people to know about you. And like all good networking opportunities, you never know who you might meet and where these introductions might lead!

Beware of Your Friends

Q. Ciao! I moved to Italy a year ago, to marry an Italian citizen last month. It has taken a year, but I am now getting over my culture shock and rollercoaster emotions to feel like I am finally settling in. My problem is that when I arrived, I became friends with a woman—also married to an Italian—at an expat meet-up and shared a lot of my transition angst with her. I invited her to my wedding, but she complained to every expat guest about how horrible her life is, and told them how I have been depressed in Italy and will really suffer when the excitement of my wedding is over. I was completely offended and shocked when my friends and family asked me "Who was that girl?" She was also the only guest who came to the wedding and did not buy us a gift.

It is true that I was feeling down when I met her and poured my heart and soul out to her. But I am adjusting: I am learning the language, I am starting to drive like the locals, and I have finally got my work permit! I am out of the fog, yet one year later she is still rude, miserable and makes no effort to speak Italian. In an expat community that seems very small, this is like a television soap opera that I did not sign up for. Any suggestions on how to politely rid my life of this negative person, yet still cope when I see her in social situations?

A. It goes without saying that friendships are a vital part of human existence. We need friends to feel connected and create that all-important sense of belonging. Not until we are removed from our existing friendships and social support network do we realize how lonely, vulnerable and insecure we can feel.

For an expatriate moving to a new country, that sense of not belonging is one of the most obvious and often painful adjustments, and something that most expatriates try to rectify as soon as possible. Expats, quite understandably, tend to quickly befriend others to help alleviate the stress of the move and unknown territory and to recreate a sense of security and belonging.

Women thrive on friendship. As a new person in town, it is impossible to immediately know everything about the people you are meeting—so do not feel guilty. Feelings of insecurity and vulnerability can tend to take charge, resulting in you potentially befriending the first person that seems nice and talks to you.

Interestingly, a study[1] in 2000 by the University of California revealed that men and women react differently to stress in a social context. Men have a tendency to either go off by themselves or engage in a highly competitive sport with other men, while women seek each other out and commiserate, either engaging in a group project or a discussion. So, women "tend and befriend"—seeking out other women to find comfort and solace—which is perhaps why expat women's coffee mornings are usually such a success.

It could be due to this innate need to have friends that expat relationships have the tendency to become extremely familiar and intense in a very short period of time. The mere commonality of being a foreigner in a community can provide a recipe for instant friendship and an immediate connection to others. And let's face it, no one can understand the mixed emotions you are experiencing like another expat woman.

Friends can outgrow one another. However, what can happen in these quickly formed expat "friendships" is that eventually one person outgrows or emotionally exceeds the other. Most newcomers will start to make an effort to get involved in their community and new culture and make a life for themselves, just as you have done. They start to get established, and once they regain their confidence

[1] http://www.apa.org/monitor/julaug00/stress.aspx

and feel comfortable in their new environment, they find that they may not need the same type of support a particular acquaintance provided at the beginning.

This "ability to stand on your own two feet" can be difficult for the other person to comprehend—they may feel jealous of your ability to "move on," settle in and create a life for yourself. They may not feel special anymore, because you have moved on and are happy in your new environment. Your ability to settle in may also draw unwanted attention to the fact that the other person is not coping so well or moving forward with her life. And this may come as a rude awakening. You might find that your "friend" is envious of you and what you have become. The only way she knows how to make herself feel better is to belittle, shock and/or offend you.

Cutting ties can be difficult. So, what next? It sounds like you would be better off without your former friend's negativity dragging you down. Friendships are supposed to be supportive, friendly and fun, not a competition or a negative experience. In the past, it may have been a one-sided relationship, with you pouring your heart out and her gaining "power" from your distress. Now that your distress has gone... more power to you!

How to sever ties? You are correct in recognizing the need to tread cautiously in a small, close-knit expat community where everybody can know everybody else's business. We suggest you be the bigger person and remain the consummate professional by not bad-mouthing this person in public, making a show of her behavior or ignoring her at social events. You probably just wish there were a magic fix to take away the pain, but unfortunately there is none. As time passes, the strength of your feelings toward her will dwindle. And most likely, given that you are both expats, one of you will probably move on to another location.

Moving forward. We really admire the way you have taken charge of your situation (in terms of your language skills, driving and work permit) and are making a go of it.

Keep moving forward and all the very best for your future.

Feeling Unwelcome

Q. My husband's job has taken us to a small, remote island community in the middle of nowhere. The population is just over one thousand people, and there is only one very expensive flight off the island each week. Needless to say, there is not much to do here. I have gone from having a full social diary back home to a life that is very limited, insular, restricting and not very social at all.

The climate is hot and harsh, which does not help. I am miserable in my part-time job: my colleagues resent me and resist my ideas. To make it even worse, the locals seem to hate the foreign community and bully us for our modern views—they even chased one expat off the island who blogged about her experiences! How can I deal with these issues and still enjoy the expat experience?

A. The fantasized notion of life on an exotic, deserted island is not always what it seems. We are sorry to hear of your situation and can empathize with you, knowing from first-hand experience just how insular and restricting some expatriate assignments can be and how isolated you must feel. However, we also commend you for maintaining your positivity and proactively seeking advice to help you improve your current situation. You have a great attitude, and all the advice in the world would be meaningless without your positive outlook and enthusiastic spirit.

Patience is a virtue. Isolation is a very common feeling within the expatriate community. Being uprooted and transplanted to a new country, to make a new home within a new and foreign culture, learn a new language (often) and meet new people takes its toll on even the most seasoned expatriate. Usually it can take anywhere from six to twelve months (or longer) to get "settled," sound out your environs, and get involved in the local and expatriate community. However, this can take a great deal longer in what appears to be a closed, seemingly unfriendly, local community. So like it or not, patience will probably need to become one of your greatest virtues. Be patient with your local community, hold your head high, and do not be intimidated. Show that you have stamina and that you are determined to make this work.

Interact with others. While it probably sounds easier said than done, we suggest that your main focus be just to try to make the best of your situation so that it is a positive and productive experience for you. Keeping motivated and making a conscious effort to engage in some form of interaction with others around you will not only prevent the feelings of isolation but will also broaden your outlook and experience. Try to set a weekly goal of speaking to a certain number of people each day or attending a local social or business event. Meeting people is the key, and keeping an open mind may lead to opportunities that you previously never noticed.

Have you considered starting your own social network? Starting a new group could help you, others who feel like you, plus others who will come to the island after you—which might be a satisfying legacy to leave one day when you move on. Starting a group takes someone with a bit of get-up-and-go to "rally the troops" and create something special, and you sound as if you have what it takes. Think about a weekly coffee morning, a dinner, a monthly luncheon, a weekly game of cards, a sports event, a yoga or Pilates class, a cooking meet-up, a book group, or whatever else is of interest to you and applicable to your environment. (See *Starting Your Own Club*)

How about charity work? Have you looked into volunteer opportunities in your community? This may be a great way to befriend the local community and dispel any preconceived ideas the locals have about you and/or the foreign population. You might even surprise yourself and make some local friends.

Make sure you are also keeping in touch with your friends and family back home—even on days when you feel sad or alone. Skype (and similar web telephone services) and email make this extremely easy to do (assuming connections are functioning in your location).

Write in a journal. You may want to keep a journal. This tends to help in a few ways. First and foremost, it can reduce stress and angst. Writing things down can help you offload frustrations and thoughts, and enable you to "see" what it is that is really bothering you. You may then be able to work at either avoiding or confronting those triggers. Instead of paying attention to the negative, journal writing can encourage you to look for the positive aspects of each day, and your journal can become an irreplaceable treasure of memories that can be looked at years from now.

Reconsider unsatisfying work. If your job is making you miserable, is it worth it? Do you absolutely need to work, or would you be able to take the rest of your time in this particular location and put it to more productive or personal use? Take some time to reevaluate your life in big-picture terms, for example: Where are you at emotionally, physically, socially, creatively and career-wise? What are your long-term goals and what do you want in the short term from your current location?

Should you have to work, then have you spoken to your manager and/or someone you trust at work about your colleagues' attitudes and asked their advice on how you could ease the tension at work? Are you trying to share lunch or after-work activities with some of your colleagues? Take a step back and assess your own behavior: are you showing genuine interest in your colleagues' lives and activities? Is there something different you could be doing to demonstrate that your intentions at work are sincere and that you truly want to add value to the team?

If you can honestly say you have tried everything and that all of your efforts seem fruitless, maybe it is time to start looking for a new role on the island or to create your own role. Could you be volunteering or starting your own business (either focused on your local market or perhaps a virtual business that deals with clients or companies abroad and has no real interaction with the local community)? Could you enroll in a distance-education course? Could you take this opportunity to indulge some long-held passion to learn a musical instrument, new sport or special craft?

Keep your head held high. Remember that old adage "All good things come to an end"? Well, so do bad things. If your positive energy wanes sometimes, remember that this too will pass. One day your stay on this island will make for an entertaining story and perhaps even provide the content for your own blog or book: think *Julie & Julia*.

In the meantime, keep a journal, nurture your self-esteem and sense of identity, befriend others on the island who might be in your same position, stay connected to the outside world so that you keep your perspective, smile, and try to find some island adventures to write about and partake in.

Household Help

Q. I am about to move from Scotland to Asia, where it seems the norm is to have household help. I am worried about this, as I have never had domestic help before and I have no idea where I would start to look for a helper and/or what a helper should or should not do. Can you please give me some insights on this topic?

A. Described by some as a perk of living an expatriate life, yes, household helpers are commonly employed by expats in many (but not all) countries. There can be many reasons for hiring a helper. The chief one being that labor is often cheaper in the country where you are living as an expat.

Some expats argue that they need a helper overseas because their housing is larger than at "home," they go through more clothes each week (due to events, functions and other activities) and/or they need someone to interpret at the markets for them or run errands that they cannot easily do themselves. Whether you subscribe to any of this reasoning or not, if the price is affordable, why not have someone help you at home so that you can spend your time doing things that might bring you more satisfaction?

Here are some of the issues to consider on the topic of household help.

Privacy and trust. While the hiring of a part-time helper can be reasonably simple, having a full-time, live-in helper can be much more complicated. Nearly every aspect of that person's life must integrate into your family's routine. It is extremely easy in many ways to have a full-time helper, but there is always some apprehension regarding privacy and trust. Having a helper look after your household means that they know the ins and outs of your family's doings, comings and goings. Helpers that live in usually have access to all the rooms and drawers, which again requires trust and leaves little to their imagination, being an outsider of the family. This can be awkward if you have secrets that you do not want shared.

That said, if you are deciding between a live-in and a day helper, many families prefer live-ins, as this means you would always have someone on hand to watch your children if you wanted or needed to go out unexpectedly (even just to buy bread or visit a neighbor). Day helpers have also been known to "hover" around you, when they have nothing to do, just so that they "look busy," whereas if live-in helpers have any spare time, they tend to retreat to their own room and leave you in peace.

Communication. Besides sharing your household, communication can also be a challenge: misunderstandings are common, especially in the beginning when your habits or preferences regarding food, cleaning and other household issues are not known to your helper. It takes a while to get to know someone and to interpret moods and body language. Different cultures interpret scenarios differently, so it takes a bit of time for you to get to know those—and equally, for your helper to get to know your nuances. Given that this would be the first time for you to have a helper, allow yourself some time to learn how to handle domestic situations. If possible, hire on a trial period first, before taking on anyone as a permanent employee.

Finding and hiring domestic help. Ways to find a helper vary by country, but the most common are via an agency, the newspaper or word of mouth. Try to find someone who comes with a personal recommendation. Helpers often advertise on supermarket notice boards or in the magazines or newsletters associated with women's clubs. Using these options sometimes works, but try to speak to one of your potential helper's (preferably expat) employers before hiring them. If you are a parent, ask other parents when you are waiting at the classroom door or ask your neighbors; your neighbors' helpers might know of someone.

In addition, notwithstanding possible language barriers, try to ask your potential helper questions that involve their detailed background information, and explain clearly your expectations and ask them for theirs. Bear in mind that most helpers will not be too forthcoming about expectations of you at their interview—aside from salary, of course—due to the understandable power imbalance in the interview situation.

Salaries for household helpers depend on what country you are in. Information is usually available via local expat websites or clubs about how much you are expected to pay for any specific location. You should always ask around among fellow expats as well, particularly among your neighbors—for it is these employers' helpers that your helper will start to befriend and compare salaries with. When you arrive, talk to someone who has been an expat for a while in the country you are in—they are usually a wealth of information regarding household help and other key aspects of settling in. Remember also to find out about the local customs and laws regarding employers' responsibilities—ranging from food responsibilities to health insurance, holidays, salary, bonuses, termination, home leave (if applicable), work hours, and so on. And it is a good idea to get a copy of your helper's passport or ID card, in case of legal issues.

Setting expectations. When a helper starts working for you, it is also highly advisable to set clear guidelines and boundaries regarding expectations, both from the employer's perspective and the employee's, and to put these expectations in writing. Setting the daily tasks in writing, on a sheet posted in the kitchen, is also a great idea. Older helpers might not be too happy to follow your schedule at first, but once they learn it (usually in the first month), they should rarely need to check it again and typically feel more comfortable about their new schedule.

Resistance to household help. From our experience, new expats (in locations where household help is affordable and readily available) who resist hiring household help so they can stay the superhero of the home are typically the expats that have the most trouble adjusting. Your quality of life *can* improve tremendously when you do not have to cook, clean or worry about piles of laundry.

So, if you think you could benefit from household help, find some—and enjoy the luxury while you can!

Chapter 2

Career and Money

Loss of Career

Q. I am forty-one years old and I am facing having to give up my architectural career because my husband has received a really good job offer in Africa. My husband's remuneration package is generous, so financially, I would not need to work in Africa. However, I cannot imagine turning into a housewife while my career is going so well. Our children are already in high school and do not need me during the day, so what would I do with all that time on my hands? I am also worried about losing touch with the job market and becoming less marketable if I do not work while we live abroad. Finding work in Africa seems daunting to me. What can I do?

A. We can very much understand your concerns. You bring up an issue that is a priority for many women. The industry-respected Brookfield Global Relocation Services' *Global Relocation Trends 2010 Survey Report* cites "spouse/partner's career" as the second-highest reason for an international assignment to be refused. The number one reason was "family concerns," which arguably often masks spouse career concerns as well. While employee-sponsored female expats are still the minority, dual-career couples are not.

In today's employment market, organizations are finding it increasingly difficult to entice employees to an overseas assignment due to their partners' career ambitions. Many dual-career couples are not willing to step off the career ladder for an overseas assignment where one partner may not be able to continue furthering their career. However, it is typically the woman who finds herself giving up her job and either looking for new work abroad (which can indeed be a daunting task) or reinventing her work to find career satisfaction.

Do your research. For accompanying partners who want to be employed abroad, finding a job may be challenging, but it is not always impossible. First, you need to be prepared. Find out as much as you can about the local situation regarding work permits, possible licensing and language concerns. Find a reputable local employment lawyer to give you sound advice. Embassies might also be able to point you in the right direction.

Find out about the international communities, business networks, professional associations and/or volunteer work options in your field of expertise. As an architect, you may be able to offer your skills to help design a charity-funded project such as a school or school extension. Even if the task is more junior than your current ability, volunteering can be a positive experience, and stories abound of trailing spouses who have gained meaningful employment or started a successful business abroad from what began as a volunteer experience.

Options and resources. Have you considered self-employment or working virtually for companies located elsewhere? A number of women write and coach about these issues, so we encourage you to seek them out. Search the Web and find resources and ideas specific to dual-career issues and portable careers abroad. Consulting an expat life coach might also help you sort through work issues.

Another idea that might appeal is to undertake further study. Online studies are widely available, and local universities sometimes have a surprising range of programs on offer in English. Most major places have international universities or at least universities with international affiliations.

Some companies offer in-house job advisors (or access to specialized job-search websites) for expatriate partners seeking work abroad or financial support in furthering their education. Some companies even have dual-career service centers that specialize in assisting partners pursuing careers abroad (which may include access to expat career coaches and/or work permit advisors).

For your interest, on this same topic, the Permits Foundation in the Netherlands is a global organization that rallies corporate support to help lobby for work permits for trailing spouses. For access to their resources and news updates, check them out online.

More resources and forums are available online, where you can find more information or network with others. We encourage you to be proactive and learn as much as you can, while keeping an open mind to new and potentially exciting opportunities for your career abroad.

Involve the entire family. In terms of your family, it is very important that you all communicate how you feel about the potential move to Africa. Each family member will have their concerns, and these concerns need to be voiced and talked through before any possible move abroad. It may even be a good idea to articulate these concerns on paper and come up with a family plan for handling issues of concern abroad. For example, what would your family's response be if your husband ends up traveling too much in his new job? Or if you struggle to find work or satisfaction abroad? Or if the children have a tough transition to their new school? Talk through possible solutions and boundaries before you leave and even discuss exit strategies, so family members know that if things turn sour abroad, the family will stick together and will not be torn apart for the sake of your husband's new job.

Finally, we suggest you explain to your husband that you would like to be as involved as much as possible in the relocation to Africa. That should make the whole process less overwhelming, and you might be able to have a say in matters that are important to you.

Good luck with your move and career.

My Job Was a Mistake

Q. I am a thirtysomething professional who came here to Switzerland as a trailing spouse. We have been living in a small town here for nearly two years, and my husband has just extended his contract for another three years. I agreed with this extension because I finally found a job and had started doing something that I felt would be meaningful to me and beneficial for my career path.

However, my job is not all that I dreamed it would be. It is quite junior compared to what I used to do, and the salary also reflects this. I have a difficult time with my manager, who is inconsistent and erratic with regards to her expectations of me. My colleagues see me as "the foreigner" and do not see the need to include me in important meetings or invite me to lunch. On the whole I am bored and lonely at work and am thinking that taking my job was a mistake. It does not give me the satisfaction, identity and social connections that I missed by not working. I am now wondering, should I stay unhappy at work or cut my losses and quit?

A. Many trailing spouses have given up their jobs to move abroad and have struggled with feelings related to the loss of a sense of achievement, identity and personal satisfaction that their previous jobs provided. This is definitely not a new phenomenon but is perhaps becoming more common due to the changing demographics of the expatriate community. Today trailing spouses tend to be more career-minded than the majority of their predecessors and more determined to maintain their identity and "be someone" abroad in their own right.

Our job or career does have a tendency to define our identity. When we suddenly stop working and "lose our identity," it is a natural reaction to reach out for something to restore our sense of self-worth, self-esteem and identity. Unfortunately, as you have discovered, taking a job abroad does not always fulfill these needs or live up to initial expectations.

Overseas experience has value. We suggest you take a step back, examine your motives and decide what is most important to you. Is just *having a job* the important factor, or is being able to account for your time or skills on your résumé your main concern?

Business literature and career guidance articles continually publicize the importance of a continuous résumé, career advancement, ongoing education and staying up-to-date in your field. In doing so, they can pressure expats—who are often building their careers laterally and/or intermittently—into thinking that they should quickly take whatever job comes their way abroad. Try not to succumb to this pressure. Step back and evaluate what is important to you.

In today's global market, what company would not benefit from a staff member who has experience living in and negotiating with other cultures? Being able to relate to and understand people from other cultures is a great skill to have, and just because your experience comes from being on the board of the International Women's Club rather than from being involved in the corporate world does not make your skills any less relevant. Do not undersell yourself and believe that just because you are not going into an office every day, you are not adding value to your résumé. Put pen to paper and you might be surprised at just how much experience your overseas posting could bring to the corporate world upon your return.

Assessing your current situation. As difficult as your job may be, remember that no job is perfect. To help with this, make a list of the pros and cons your new job gives you (both short-term and long-term). Try to figure out just how important having a *job* is for you. Think about your salary expectations and the status having a job gives you too. Then try to ascertain how important *this particular job* is for you, right here, right now.

If you decide that having a job is indeed important to you, but not necessarily your current job, have you thought about a virtual job, where you can be based from home but be working for companies elsewhere? Or if your strong preference is to find a job located where you are living, consider the old adage that it is often easier to find a job when you have a job. Employers tend to find potential employees more attractive if they are already employed. So perhaps try proactively networking now for a new job, before handing in your resignation letter.

Improving work relations. If you decide that your current job *is* important to you, then your focus probably needs to be more on how to improve things at work rather than how you can justify leaving. For example, how can you improve your relationship with your manager? Do you have a clear job description? Are you being proactive and asking for more interesting tasks to add to your current responsibilities? Can you learn any tips about how best to interact with your manager from watching and/or talking to your colleagues?

As for your colleagues, if they see you as "the foreigner," think what you can do to win them over. You can choose to keep things the way they are or you can choose to make changes. If you really want to fit in and you really do make an effort, you might be surprised... slowly but surely your colleagues might include you in their inner circle. Be patient.

Thinking big picture. If you could do *anything*, what would you do and why? Does this particular job match in some way those aspirations? Is there something else you could do while you are a trailing spouse that would provide the feeling of satisfaction, social connection, stimulation and identity you might be seeking?

Another idea: have you considered seeking advice from a life coach? A professional coach might not only be able to help you work through your current dilemma, but also offer some insights for your future career plans.

We wish you all the best with your career decisions.

Work-Life Balance

Q. Nearly a year ago, I was transferred here to Taiwan to take up an exciting role with my company. However, I have a problem: I cannot unplug from my work and I am struggling with my unhealthy work-life balance. I feel guilty when I go on vacation and find myself checking email every day, sometimes waking up at the crack of dawn to work before my husband and children wake up, just so that I am not accused of slacking off at the office. The last thing I want is to get fired for poor performance, and the fact that I have already disrupted my family to move here means I cannot afford to fail. I cannot seem to let go of work and I am missing quality time with my family. What should I do?

A. We understand your feeling of not being able to let go. As an employed female expatriate, you feel pressure from both sides: your workplace and your family. Work-life balance issue is currently a much-debated topic, especially among expats—and even more so among females working on international assignments.

The burden of responsibility. Women in general tend to fulfill multiple roles, and those holding senior expatriate positions are no exception. They are the breadwinner, wife and mother, and they tend to assume complete responsibility for all of the obstacles and negative emotions faced by the rest of the family. We do not know many women who can let go of this sense of responsibility, regardless of how senior they are at work. Instinctively, women tend to be the ones who notice and worry about how each family member is feeling: which family members are excited about the new move, which ones are angry, and which ones just want to pack up and go back home.

Getting fired is unusual after having been sent abroad, so try not to worry about this unnecessarily. Expatriate relocations are an expensive business, and your company chose you to move abroad because they believe in you and are confident you are capable to do your job. According to the Brookfield Global Relocation Services' *Global Relocation Trends 2010 Survey Report*, only six percent of assignments fail, and of these, more fail from spouse/partner/family concerns than from poor employee performance.

Everyone needs a break. Employer-sponsored expats are typically dedicated, career-minded individuals who are inclined to put in long hours. However, all work and no play can cause breakdowns, which is not good for you or your company. All employees need vacations, including the senior ones like you. So plan your holiday, advise your team and key stakeholders that you are taking a vacation, make the necessary arrangements so that your responsibilities are covered, set up your "out of office" automatic email responses—then actually go and take your well-deserved, family holiday!

Leave your laptop behind. If you still need to rationalize your lack of email activity, remind yourself that the purpose of a vacation is to take a break—for you to take a break from the office and for the office to take a break from you. Even the best managers need to give their team members some space to breathe from time to time and a chance to exercise their own decision-making abilities. The *Oxford Concise Dictionary* defines vacation as a "fixed period of cessation from work"—so do not work, do not think about work, just relax, recharge your batteries, spend quality time with those you love and engage in activities you enjoy.

If you are disciplined enough to leave your laptop at home when you go away with your family but you still feel inclined to take your PDA, set some boundaries for yourself. Remember that you can usually turn off the email noise alerts—and even turn the phone off altogether. Set yourself parameters, and only turn your phone on in the time slot you have set yourself.

Talk to your partner. Also, remember to communicate your feelings and concerns to your spouse. The working partner usually does not always give the "full story" to their spouse to avoid heated discussions at home. Hiding information and certain feelings does not contribute to a healthy relationship, especially when one-half of the partnership is feeling overwhelmed with too much responsibility and pressure. Sometimes, baring your soul to your partner can not only be therapeutic, to help get rid of those secret feelings that have tied your stomach in knots every day, but it can also help your partner to understand why you may have been tense, despondent or not as relaxed as you normally would be. Who knows, maybe a good debrief and a belly laugh with your partner might be just what the doctor ordered to help you release that tension and start focusing one hundred percent on enjoying your holiday!

Get support from others. It sounds as if you probably cannot unplug well even when you are *not* on vacation. This is another area to focus on. Seek strategies for easing this ongoing sense of tug-of-war inside your mind, between work, family and "you" time.

Are you a member of any social networks in your community? If not, start looking into local social or business networks to find some support. The friendship and camaraderie garnered from these networks can provide an invaluable social outlet as well as practical support. More importantly, such groups also provide emotional nurturance, affirmation of worth, advice and companionship. Having peers in the same situation as yourself can help you see just what is normal—and what is excessive anxiety on your part. You might also want to think about finding a mentor in your company—or elsewhere in your industry. Ideally, find someone with whom you can discuss how your core values and beliefs affect your adjustment to an international move, and talk about how best to tackle any issues in this area.

A few final tips. Perhaps also consider reexamining your expectations. Learn what is controllable in your life and what is not, and if you find a discrepancy, try to adjust your expectations accordingly. This could save you considerable anguish and unhappiness.

Finally, do not expect your company to anticipate your feelings and concerns. Develop a collaborative relationship with your contacts at the company. Help them to understand your circumstances and work with you to structure your work time so that it *does* end when you leave the office each day.

Believe in yourself—you can perform well without working 24/7. Work is important, but not nearly as important as the loving family waiting for you at home every evening.

Lack of Respect at Work

Q. I have only been in the Middle East four months and I am struggling with the way I am treated in the office. I am a senior manager with a European company. I understand that women here have a different "status" to women back home in Europe, but how can I do my job with all these impediments? I have spoken to Human Resources at our head office, but they think I am being a bit melodramatic. I am at a loss and feel like I am starting to lose control, my temper, and the little bit of respect I had gained in the office. Your thoughts would be much appreciated.

A. It sounds as if you are in a bit of a bind. We are not sure which is worse: the fact that you are a professional female feeling restricted by a male-dominated culture or that members of your Human Resources (HR) department are not paying attention to your genuine concerns and trying better to help you. We think you have every right to be angry.

Talk to HR again. Figures quoted vary greatly, but most times we read that a company-sponsored expatriate posting costs between US$250,000 and $750,000+ per year. So, companies cannot afford to ignore genuine expatriate employee issues. If they do, they run the risk of a premature repatriation and the very high expense involved—directly, with the repatriating employee, and indirectly, in terms of disgruntled staff and an unproductive office. If you have not already done so, try targeting different people in HR, or allies you might have who could influence people in HR to both listen to you and support you.

Learn all you can about local protocol. If you have not received any already, perhaps ask for some gender-specific cross-cultural training from your company or from a local professional consultancy. To do your job well, you need to be prepared and have some tried-and-tested strategies for operating successfully in male-dominated cultures. Technical job skills are one thing, but you also need gender-specific information. You need to be aware of the intricacies of both the social and business culture in your new location.

If you are unable to receive relevant training, we suggest you go online and research as much as you can about the country's culture and general business etiquette—both for general operations and for specific issues that perhaps have been faced by those who have gone before you.

Knowledge is power, which can equal success in the workplace. If the local culture demands wearing certain clothing to be successful, then you need to know this in advance and consider it. All efforts to learn the local culture, the office culture and any relevant religious customs will not only help you personally, but they most likely will also help you indirectly to gain more respect from your staff—just by your interest and knowledge in this area.

Enhance your credibility. Female managers seconded to male-dominated locations need to be presented as highly qualified professionals from the moment they arrive in the host location. This gives the female manager credibility and respect in the eyes of her colleagues. In addition to communicating your credentials up front and in writing, wherever possible, try to gain public endorsement from male colleagues at your company headquarters as well.

Next time your management team members are in town, ask them to organize a staff presentation where a high-ranking male in the company introduces you. This enables the host nationals to see that you are highly respected within the company. In some male-centric societies, the idea that a female was chosen for the position over a man already raises her status and affords her the respect she deserves. Use this to your advantage.

At the same time, be very aware of damaging your credibility by doing something that undermines your authority in a patriarchal society. For example, while tasks such as using the photocopier or making yourself a cup of tea in the office back home might be considered a sign of independence, in your current location, these tasks might be reserved for lower-level women and employees, so these tasks could be weakening your seniority status.

Be the best you can be. A knowledgeable, confident, competent manager has much better prospects of garnering respect in her new location than a timid, nervous manager with noticeable gaps in her knowledge base. Focus on listening and learning every day—be as intelligent and as street-savvy as you can be. This will help you gain respect in the workplace; it should also serve to increase you own self-esteem and personal confidence, in all areas of your new life.

Find mentors. Mentors are a fabulous idea, so you might want to find one for yourself—someone you trust and respect, either within your office or outside. Use this person to bounce ideas off and to vent frustrations to along the way.

Adapt as best you can. And finally, an important point to remember: you cannot change the traditions and beliefs of a centuries-old culture just because it does not fit your own cultural paradigm. Try to adapt as best you can.

Know when to move on. If you are feeling truly uncomfortable and struggling to see the benefit of working in such an environment, do not be afraid to tell headquarters. It is your responsibility and duty to your organization to advise them if you decide that you cannot function productively in this particular location. Ideally, they should appreciate you for your honesty and help you to transition home or elsewhere, to a location more suited to your style of leadership.

Be sure to explain the situation personally plus submit a formal report with professional suggestions for the next assignee to overcome the issues you have encountered. And remember to schedule an interview with your HR manager and/or direct report manager to debrief.

Like anything in life, give it your best shot but if it does not work out, you are not a failure for wanting to move on to something better elsewhere. Do what is right for you.

I Need More Than Coffee

Q. I am a professional woman and have decided to take a break from my job as a political advisor to the United Nations to join my husband on sabbatical here in Portugal for two years. We knew about the move five months prior so had enough time to research, plan and get excited about our new adventure. I made a list of all the activities I wanted to do during these two years and contacted many of the international clubs before arriving. I daydreamed about my well-deserved break from work, the time I would get to spend with my husband and all the things I was going to do.

However, we have been here for six months and I cannot believe how lost and dissatisfied I feel. I am shocked and embarrassed to feel this way, as I genuinely thought I would get enough stimulation from my surroundings, supplemented by the local expat club activities. I realize now that I need more than coffee. I know this is a turnaround from my initial plans, but it is very obvious to me that I cannot continue down this path for much longer with my sanity intact. My visa does not allow me to work here. Any suggestions?

A. As you have discovered, the transition from full-time employment to not working at all can be a difficult one. Take heart, however, in the fact that many professional women before you have taken time off and had a rewarding and valuable experience, whether overseas or at home.

After the "honeymoon." It is not uncommon for the nonworking partner to feel lost after relocating. The first six months are often referred to as the "honeymoon period" of expatriate life, when you are busy setting up your home, exploring your new city and discovering who you are outside of your own country. Yet once the final boxes are unpacked and you have visited the last museum on your list, "real life" begins, which can be quite a crash back down to earth. Quite quickly, the glamor and excitement of expat life can wear off, and you are left trying to put some meaning back into your life.

If you want to stay with your husband in Portugal and abide by your visa restrictions, you can choose to spend the next year and a half either fighting your decision to take time off or accepting your situation and using your time wisely. Your stay is not forever, you do have an end date, so do not be so hard on yourself. There are many things you can do over the next eighteen months that do not have to involve just coffee mornings.

Plan of action. First of all, we suggest you dig up the list of to-do activities you wrote before arrival. These were obviously things that motivated and inspired you when you were excited about having time off. Review your list and see which things are possible and interesting to you now. If you can only look at that list with a tired, lost face, then go out, get some exercise, take a shower and come back to look at the list with new, positive eyes.

Choose three items that stimulate you the most and make them this week's project. Along with physical exercise, being proactive is the best way to ward off depression, self-pity and negativity—especially for a goal-oriented person.

Second, look into volunteer work, perhaps in a field that would enhance your credibility as a political advisor with the UN or perhaps in a completely unrelated area that has always interested you. Alternatively, have you thought about the possibility of furthering your education via online or long-distance courses? You said that you cannot work locally, but can you do some home-based work projects with your previous employer or any other employer willing for you to work virtually, which may not require a change to your Portuguese visa?

As a political advisor, you most likely have very good interpersonal and written communication skills. Consider using these skills to write a how-to book about your location or about any other area of your expertise. There are always new angles for existing books—and many gaps in the marketplace for new book ideas. Getting a book published is also easier than it used to be, with the advent of print-on-demand self-publishing companies that are only too happy to print anything you might like to write. If you have ever nurtured an unfulfilled dream of being a published author, maybe now is your chance to prove what you can do.

Third, if despite your best efforts, you cannot escape the fact that you are a high achiever who must have daily deadlines and goals, then create some tasks and deadlines for yourself each day. Before you go to bed each evening, know exactly which tasks you need to complete the next day, remembering to include health and well-being activities as well as activities for your sanity.

Make networking pay off. The next step is to find the "right" expat clubs or local associations for you to join—because, coffee or no coffee, there really is great value in building supportive networks for yourself abroad. You never know when you might need someone, now or in the future, for work contacts, social contacts or help in an emergency. If you cannot find your ideal group, start your own. (See *Starting Your Own Club*)

When you network, remember to have some business cards (yes, you can make your own!) with a professional title on them and target the business-related groups. Meeting like-minded individuals should not only provide some inspiration and understanding but will also provide you with support and friendship.

It sounds as if you are an ambitious person who expects results in all that you do. So, set yourself some direction and a sense of purpose each day—and live it! While it might sometimes feel like a burden, if you think about it, it really is a privilege to be able to have the time and financial support to enjoy and experience another culture and all that it has to offer, without the pressure of working.

We hope you make the most of your time abroad and come home enriched, refreshed and inspired.

Starting a Business

Q. I have been here in Europe for eight months, and I am now at a point where I have accepted that I can no longer work in my old profession and need to look for alternatives. I would love to start a business and I have a few ideas, but which idea should I pursue and how do I start a business abroad?

A. It is fabulous to hear that you have worked through your job-search frustrations and that you are now ready to "think outside of the box" to create some new career options. You will need all the energy that you can muster for your new entrepreneurial pursuit, so it is great that you have accepted your situation and cleared your mind of any unhelpful career-related resentment you might have harbored for moving abroad.

Choosing your business. Tamara Monosoff in her book *Your Million Dollar Dream* outlines three primary paths that entrepreneurs follow to find the business that is "right" for them:

1. *Do what you know*, which leverages on your current knowledge base and your existing network of contacts.

2. *Do what others do:* namely, become a franchisee and take advantage of the systems and market-testing that others have done before you.

3. *Solve a problem.* Create a "new" product or service to meet a need in the marketplace—a route which might or might not have anything to do with your previous skill set or career experience.

To help you decide which of these paths to follow, and which specific business to pursue, here are some more factors to consider before you launch your new business.

Your personality. The first thing to consider is how well your new business idea matches your personality. The reason for this is that although starting a business can be an exciting ride, the ride is typically a rollercoaster of ups and downs and will require a genuine passion and boundless energy on your part. You will find it difficult to put in the hours and commitment required if your heart is not fully behind your business and you are not willing to make sacrifices on a day-to-day basis. Ask yourself:

✳ What are your values in life?

✳ Does the business fit with your values?

✳ What do you love doing?

✳ Are you passionate enough about your business idea to work without pay for a year (or more) if necessary?

Your lifestyle. The second aspect to assess is how well your new business idea complements your current expatriate lifestyle. Ask yourself:

✳ Can you pursue all (or part of) your business idea now, in your expat location?

✳ Can you continue your business if you move locations? (Your answer need not be yes, but you do need to think about this before you embark on your venture, in case it does make a difference which business you choose.)

✳ Can you juggle the hours the business requires with other personal or family commitments?

* Can the business run without you, if you take extended and/or frequent vacations?

* If you need team members to help you, where will those team members be based, and can you manage them from your current location abroad?

* Can you legally work or stay in your current location while you are establishing your business?

Business questions. Just as there are many different business ideas, there are also many different ways to set up your business. Questions to ask include the following:

* Should you set up in your current location?

* Do you need a local partner to start your business, either to comply with local legalities or to help you find the contacts or distribution channels you need to make it a success?

* Can your work be performed virtually and can you set up in your home location?

* Can you start a business in your home country, then work on it remotely? If so, will you operate it fully right now or just start the building-block phase of the business so that if and when you return home, the business will be all set up and ready to move forward?

* Do you set up a sole proprietorship, a larger company structure, a business or family trust structure, or some other structure?

After you have researched as much as possible about your chosen business type and your setup options, it would be wise to consult a reputable lawyer as well as an array of relevant business advisors, to help you plan your next steps.

Business advisors. Any credible person who could counsel you on your new business could be considered a business advisor. Ideally you should seek out several, such as some of the following:

* Friends or peers who have set up businesses in your current location, particularly anyone whose industry matches yours, as they should understand the hurdles and challenges you might face.

* Friends or peers in other locations (both at home and abroad) who can share with you what they have learned and help guide you through potential obstacles.

* Local or national government authorities, who can advise you how to start a business in your new location.

* Members of local business associations, who often gather at networking functions and may be able to offer practical advice from their own experiences.

* Members of online entrepreneur support groups, to encourage you and offer ideas about how to overcome challenges you might encounter.

* A reputable lawyer (perhaps both at home and abroad), to ensure you have considered all legal aspects of your business.

* A reputable accountant, to talk you through any common mistakes and to check that you understand the tax, business and accounting obligations of whatever locale in which you choose to set up your business.

Business plan. Central to any business start-up is the need for a well-constructed business plan. Before you make up those business cards, remember to think through the following, as a minimum:

* What are your goals for starting your business?

* What is the business vision?

* How will your business make money?

* What investment will be required from you before you will turn a profit?

* What will you do if it takes longer for your business to be profitable than you first projected?

* If the primary goal is not to make money but to develop your skill set for your career track, what milestones must you reach and by when to know that you have been successful in your efforts?

* Who will be your customers and have you surveyed your target audience?

* If you have a partner or family, will they support you in your business venture?

As you can see, there is much to consider when starting a business, but do not let this overwhelm you. If you are truly passionate about your business concept, you will answer all of the questions you need to and know deep down in your heart how to embark on setting up your business abroad.

If, however, you decide that you are not passionate about your concept, then now is the time to be honest and to either find a new idea or try to adapt your concept so that you could become passionate about it. Your first business idea does not need to be your greatest, but you do need to be zealous enough about it to want to jump over all the hurdles that you will encounter on your road to potential success.

Best of luck with your entrepreneurial plans!

Confused About Finances

Q. My husband has been offered the possibility of a position in the Middle East. We are seriously considering it, but we are a little unclear on the financial aspect. The contract looks healthy, but I am wondering about the "hidden costs" of living and earning abroad. Friends have told us to be wary of issues such as local taxes abroad, pension schemes, exchange rates, saving accounts, and so on. I feel out of my depth, confused and overwhelmed. Can you please help?

A. You are very wise to be cautious and curious as to how an expatriate posting can affect your financial position. As you have intimated, there are plenty of factors you should take into consideration, both in your host destination and your home country, with regards to your finances. It would be prudent to do some homework and understand what exactly an overseas posting could mean for you monetarily, before making the move.

Sadly, many expatriates misinterpret their expat package, get caught up in the high life and/or overindulge with fine dining, exotic holidays and carefree spending while abroad. This does little to help them get ahead financially in the long term. Some expats even return home to find themselves in financial difficulty as a result.

However, with some forward thinking and informed planning, an international assignment can definitely be a positive (or, in some cases, lucrative) experience. Here are a few important considerations:

Seek advice. First and foremost, we suggest contacting a reputable financial advisor. Shop around for someone who specializes in expatriate assignments and, if possible, someone who is acquainted with the fiscal system in both your host country and your home country. (Alternatively, you may need a financial advisor in both locations.) Meet a few advisors to compare advice and find someone you feel comfortable with. Often first-time meetings are obligation free, and it can be valuable to hear the perspectives of different reputable advisors to help you understand various implications.

A good advisor should be able to guide you on what is best for your current assets (bank accounts, stocks or shares, properties, loan repayments and the like) and how to manage these from abroad. They should also be able to make suggestions on how best to utilize your expatriate income, taking into consideration important aspects like taxes (at home and abroad), exchange rates, and local policies with regards to moving and holding money. Some countries, such as China, have strict policies on moving money outside of the country, which is compounded by the nonconvertible Chinese currency. Issues such as becoming a nonresident of your home country for tax purposes, setting up offshore bank accounts and participating in offshore investment schemes may also be of interest.

Bear in mind that some advisors might recommend strategies for you to implement before you move abroad, so it is a good idea to seek advice as soon as possible (and perhaps meet up with a knowledgeable bank manager as well). Then, try to maintain regular contact once you have relocated (especially after you have a better idea of your true cost of living and leftover disposable income abroad). Perhaps your financial advisor might even have a representative in your new part of the world.

Make the most of your current assets. Make sure you consider how to best preserve or grow your existing assets while you are away. For example, if you are moving out of your own home to move overseas, you may want to consider the financial gains and expenses associated with renting versus selling your property. Be wise about what you do with the rental income, and be aware of taxes and potential costs with both options. What about your current savings accounts at home? If these will be inactive while you are away, have you considered putting a lump sum of cash into a fixed deposit or high-interest account?

Also, be smart about managing currency risk. If possible, get in touch with a colleague who is working in your host country and find out what they do in terms of bank accounts and so forth. Do you have a pension or retirement savings scheme in place? If you are new to the company, check with your company if they have a scheme in place. Alternatively, a financial advisor may suggest an offshore pension plan, which can also make the most of exchange rates.

Get street-smart. Think local. Think about where you will get paid and how you will get paid. It is not uncommon to be paid a percentage in local currency and the remainder in your home currency. Will you set up a local bank account? As a foreigner, are you allowed to? What is the best way for you to deal with the exchange rates? For example, some people need to consider and plan for being paid or renting a home in one currency but paying bills or mortgages in a different currency.

What about your credit cards? Can you qualify for local ones? Where and in what currency will these be paid? What are the terms and conditions of local credit cards, and how do these differ from those in your home country?

Cover yourself. If you have global assets (such as offshore bank accounts, property and/or income in two countries), it might be in your best interest to have a local will document drawn up. This is essential when you are moving to a Middle Eastern country, for example, where Sharia law prevails. Check the up-to-date laws in your host country and make sure you understand what will happen to your assets should anything happen to you as the main income earner. Will your family members be able to access bank accounts and credit cards? Will one of you be permitted to stay in the country, take the children and/or leave the country in the event that something happens to the other one of you?

Also investigate medical insurance. Most companies will provide health insurance to expatriates on official assignments, but this is not guaranteed, and the policy may not adequately cover your family. Check your medical insurance coverage carefully. If you need to find your own medical insurer, ask around for reputable providers, request quotes (these are usually available online), then compare costs, policy coverage and the "fine print." This is important because quality medical care in some locations (such as the United States) can be phenomenally expensive. Ensure that you have adequate coverage (which ideally should include emergency evacuation, if you are concerned about the medical facilities in your new location).

Wise expatriates also have a contingency bank account for easy access to money in case of emergency.

Hidden costs. Many expats accept a job overseas without realizing all of the "hidden costs" abroad and thus the full financial implications of an overseas relocation. In addition to the costs already outlined, hidden costs might include the following:

∗ *Accommodation.* Will the employer pay part or all of this? Will the employer component fluctuate? Will you have to pay for your own utilities or maintenance? Will you be given a choice in terms of your preferred property options and/or location? If not, and you would like to live elsewhere, can you afford to pay the difference? Will your employer pay if you need to move homes during the assignment? If not, can you afford to?

* *Schools.* What are the options and associated costs? How much will your employer pay? If your employer has a school fee threshold, is that negotiable? If your assignment ends abruptly, what help is given to transition your children to a new school elsewhere or, alternatively, to continue to pay the existing school fees until the end of the school year? (The latter can be a critical consideration for students in their senior years.)

* *Transportation.* Is a car provided? Does the provision include maintenance, fuel and insurance? Is an annual flight home included for you and your family?

* *Social costs.* How much does it cost to join local social groups? How much will you spend socializing and dining out? Although such activities might sound like luxuries, for a newcomer thrown into a foreign city, a budget for socializing is important if you are going to successfully establish social networks and support systems in your new home.

Weigh your options. You come across as a very switched-on expat-to-be, and we believe you are absolutely correct in doing your homework before you agree to any potential assignment abroad. The general rule of thumb in areas that are new to you is "Ask, ask, ask and research, research, research"—which is exactly what you are doing.

If you do go abroad, the same savings and investment principles apply as at home: be mindful of your income and your spending, and try your best to achieve the financial goals you set for yourself. Living the high life is fun in the short term, but saving and investing will make you feel much better about yourself in the long run, just as it does back home. Try it!

Show Me the Money

Q. Six months ago, I was in a great job back home in London. No, I was not a career professional as such, but I was paid very well. I agreed to leave my job because everything about my husband's new posting to Malaysia sounded incredibly exciting, and it was never really an option in my mind to commute or to separate from my husband of three years. However, I am not coping well with financial dependence: I feel guilty asking for money, and I feel that my husband is using his control of his money as some sort of power play. We are arguing daily about this, which is unlike us, and we are not a very happy couple. Please help.

A. Your situation touches on a very typical sense of loss and change in the dynamics of a relationship when one person in the partnership becomes financially dependent. This issue not only affects expatriate couples, but anyone who becomes financially dependent (stay-at-home parents being a perfect example).

Power and control. There is a reason those who have money are usually smiling: money is a very powerful commodity. Money can buy a sense of freedom—to buy a meal, to own a laptop and to know that you can board a bus or a plane and leave an unhappy situation at any time. The person who controls the money, in many cases, controls the freedom.

This sense of control is especially important to acknowledge in an expatriate assignment, where a change in environment, employment status, culture, friendships and so many other changes in everyday living can often leave new expats feeling extremely out of control. Losing financial control as well can be another major blow to what may be an already fragile sense of self-esteem.

In this day and age, most women work or have worked and have therefore had their own source of income and relative financial independence. Losing this can be an incredibly difficult transition for a newly unemployed or underemployed expatriate woman. Add the frustration, in your case, that your usually supportive partner is not being particularly sensitive to your feelings, and it is understandable why you are reaching out for help. So how can you feel better?

Work brings satisfaction. We encourage you to further explore the possibility of finding either paid or voluntary employment in your new location. Granted, you may have already looked or you may not have access to the proper work visa, so try to think creatively about the whole concept of "work."

For example, could you work virtually, for a client back home or elsewhere? What kind of work might you be able to do, including volunteer or intern work in a new field of interest? This work might not be full-time or what you were doing back home, it might not pay very much (if anything at all), but it might just give you back that sense of independence and satisfaction you had when you were working back home—and thus make you feel more in control of your overall situation.

Remember also to take pride in whatever you are doing to help settle your family unit into your new environment. Do not belittle your importance or input into the relationship, just because your current role is not technically a "paid" position.

Your own bank account. If you have not already done so, consider opening your own bank account, if legally feasible. This way it would be possible for you to transfer the money you have agreed you need for day-to-day spending directly to your account each time your husband gets paid. This should help to alleviate your sense of guilt and the embarrassment of needing to "ask" your husband for money for the most basic things. If you cannot get your own bank account, agree that each time your husband gets paid, he brings home a specific amount of cash and from then on, you are responsible for looking after it.

A workable budget. We also suggest the two of you sit down and draw up a household budget. If you have never done this, be warned that to be honest and see exactly what a household's financial capacity really is can be a very confronting process. Start with the essentials, such as accommodation costs, utilities, groceries, transportation and essential bills. Then work out how much you want to save each month, so your long-term financial position is not negatively affected by your new posting. Then budget for the fun stuff, like holidays and exotic getaways. After that you should be aiming to come to some sort of realistic agreement about how much you really can spend on a daily basis, so you can spend this amount guilt-free.

Uncovering hidden issues. With regards to your relationship, it is important to ask yourself why your husband might be controlling the money. If he is doing it consciously, why do you think this is happening? Does he have a pattern of wanting to control things between the two of you in the past? If yes, well, that habit might be the one that needs identifying and breaking. If not, why do you think he would start trying to control you now? Do you think he is feeling out of control in this new foreign environment and therefore trying to compensate by gaining increased control at home? Or are your own issues with possibly lowered self-esteem and/ or financial dependence clouding your views of your relationship, especially in terms of finances?

If your husband is not consciously trying to limit your freedom by controlling the finances, why do you think he is unable to see the effect this is having on you and on your relationship? Is it because he may genuinely not appreciate that you do need money to spend each day (for example, on transport, food, outings, meet-ups with friends and other commitments)? Is it because he may not yet grasp just how much things cost in your new location, and his original idea of how much you would need each day does not match the reality of your day-to-day life? Is it because your arguments about money have now made him (or both of you) very defensive about the topic, so that any new discussion is really just a rerun of a previous argument, at least in his mind (or for both of you)? Or does he genuinely have concerns that the household spending is more than is sustainable on his current income?

Whatever his reasoning, you need to communicate with your husband about the impact these finance issues are having on your relationship, and sooner rather than later. You may want to discuss with him the idea of establishing a budget and even meet with an independent, professional financial advisor.

If these ideas do not work, or perhaps even if they do, we recommend that the two of you consider seeing some sort of relationship counselor—to help you both deal with the communication issues that have prolonged this tense situation for six months already. This tactic should hopefully strengthen your relationship so that it survives not only this issue, but the myriad of other relationship issues you may face in the future—either at home or abroad.

All the very best!

No Money Left

Q. In a few months' time, my partner and I will be returning to home base. We have enjoyed postings in Madrid, Berlin, Santiago and now Cairo. We have indulged in amazing holidays, eaten at spectacular restaurants and basically had a lifestyle that was second to none. The problem now is that this upcoming move home has made us realize we have no more than two months' salary saved in our joint bank account, which is virtually nothing. This is causing us both great anxiety, as we now see that we have been a little careless with our impressive salaries abroad and we are concerned we have not set ourselves up properly for the future. What can we do?

A. Congratulations for recognizing that you need to take more proactive steps to achieve the future you seek. There are six key financial scenarios that couples tend to fall into, that move them to the point of frustration or a breakdown in the relationship. In many cases, more than one scenario is present. Identify which of the following are true for your relationship:

* No personalized spending plan.

* No *agreed-upon* personalized spending plan.

* No *clearly defined* short-, medium- or long-term financial goals.

* No *agreed-upon*, clearly defined short-, medium- or long-term financial goals.

* No structure set up to carry out what has been agreed upon.

* A lack of commitment by one or both partners to do what it will

take to reach the financial future that has been envisioned.

In terms of what you can do now, do not despair—there is plenty you can do to set yourselves up for a bright future. None of these steps are magic fixes, but if you commit to them, they will help to alleviate some of your anxiety and reassure you that you are getting back on track to achieving what you want for the future.

Step 1: Take responsibility and be accountable. You and your partner both need to accept responsibility for the joint spending of the past and realize that you will only change your joint habits if you work together. By encouraging and supporting each other in doing what is needed, not only will your stress levels be reduced, you will find it easier to reach your individual and joint goals.

Step 2: Identify spending triggers. Apart from buying the essentials, what has triggered you to spend money in the past? Is it a sense that your income is never-ending and therefore it has never needed to be monitored? Is it due to the influence of your peers? Is it due to habit—for example, have you a weekend routine that starts at the department stores, then moves to your favorite restaurant for lunch, followed by an afternoon or evening of entertainment with friends, at somewhere super expensive? Or have you spent money because it has made you feel better?

Step 3: Visualize the future. Take some time to think about what you most value and/or enjoy in life? What do you most want to have, whom do you most want to be, what will your close personal relationships look like, where will you be and what will you be doing one, five and ten years from now?

Step 4: Establish goals. Set goals that will help you to create your vision(s) of the future. Goals are the tangible benchmarks you identify that need to be accomplished to achieve your vision.

Goals need to be distinguished from *tasks*—those actions we need to take to keep our lives running smoothly, like paying the bills, servicing the car, and all of the things that do not lead directly to fulfilling our our life's *vision*. Goals must be attainable, be measurable and have time frames. For example, I will pay off my credit cards within six months, or starting today, I will set aside $100 per week until I build an emergency fund equal to three months' basic living expenses.

Brainstorm a list of goals that will get you closer to your vision(s). Then rank the goals you have listed, agree on priorities, and categorize the priorities by time. For example: immediate (within the next twelve months), short-term (one to five years), and long-term (more than five years away).

Step 5: Create a spending plan. Get into the habit of designing an annual spending plan to support your short and long term goals. A spending plan is different from a traditional budget, in that it is not just based on last year's expenditures but sets new figures, based on your new homework, experience and priorities. If, for instance, an exotic family vacation is a goal for the year and it is to be paid for in addition to your "usual" annual travel expenses, your total estimate for this category will be larger than last year and will require you to reduce spending in other categories.

When you fill in figures for the spending plan, you begin by listing all of your monthly or annual commitments and then move on to discretionary expenses. By planning out how you envision spending your money before you actually spend it, you should be able to reduce the frequency of or eliminate those spending triggers you may have identified in step two. The benefit for your relationship is that you will engage in genuine discussions about financial capability, and you will be making joint decisions about how to work together to achieve your vision(s) for the future.

Step 6: Review spending regularly. Track your spending as best you can and review it against the spending plan on a quarterly or six-month basis. This will allow you to make adjustments as you move through the calendar year. Review your goals annually to inform your next annual spending plan.

Step 7: Train your mind. A Neuro-Linguistic Programming (NLP) professional might argue that if you train your mind to believe you are struggling with your finances, then that is exactly what will happen. Instead, they might suggest that if you train your mind to believe you are in control of your finances and that you have the power to say no when you previously would have spent money, then that instead will be your outcome. We suggest you try training your mind to support you in your financial commitments, rather than to drag you down.

Step 8: Get professional help. One of your first tasks on arrival at home base should be to find yourselves a reputable financial planner. In addition, you may also find it useful to engage a life coach, either now in your current location or once you arrive home, who can help you clarify your vision of the future, motivate you and support you in taking action. A counselor may also be appropriate, depending on what your triggers for spending money have been in the past. In short, the more help and support you seek, the higher the likelihood you will move forward with your vision of a brighter financial future.

Here's wishing you a fast, sustainable financial recovery!

Special thanks to Jennifer A. Patterson, CFP® (US), CIMC™, CIMA®, TEP for helping with the original website version of this confession. Jennifer is the managing director of Patterson Partners Ltd. (www.patterson-partners.com), an international wealth management firm that specializes in cross-border financial planning. She is also the author of When Families Cross Borders: A Guide for Internationally Mobile People *and she contributed to the finance chapter of Jeanne A. Heinzer's* Living Your Best Life Abroad.

Chapter 3

Raising Children

Pregnant, Far from Home

Q. We have been in Vietnam for four months now and so far so good—especially because I have now received approval on my application to open my own counseling practice here, which is very exciting. However, I just found out that I am pregnant!

My husband and I are really happy about having a baby, but I am petrified about giving birth here, within a medical system I do not know and without the support of my family. Part of me wants to pull the plug on our assignment and return home, but I know pregnancy can play havoc with your hormones, so I was hoping you could give me some rational thoughts about what to do.

A. Congratulations on your pregnancy and for the green light on your work paperwork. Your counseling practice sounds like a flexible career option that might allow you to juggle work around your pregnancy and new motherhood, which is a great situation to be in.

Second, take a deep breath, have a seat, and try not to get ahead of yourself. The most important thing to do is to find out the facts.

Getting informed. Research, research, research—get as knowledge-able as you can about pregnancy, childbirth, and what services and facilities are available in your new location. Buy books about having a baby, visit reputable gynecologists and hospitals, speak to expats, speak to locals, and search for as much information as possible online. Once you feel you have all the information you need, then you can begin to make some rational and informed decisions.

The value of asking around the expatriate community for the lowdown on giving birth in your new city cannot be underestimated. There is sure to be an expat mothers group set up. Track them down and ask them for all the information they can share—which I am sure will be plenty. Join the group if you can and start working on establishing your support networks. They will be invaluable.

Be prepared for cultural differences in terms of bedside manner and advice. Some gynecologists ask you one hundred questions at each visit. Others ask only a few... but arguably the most important few are enough to take good care of you. Again, your mothers group may be able to offer some insight into the differences and how to overcome them if necessary. As mentioned above, actually get out and visit the medical facilities and speak to the specialist staff. It is important to feel comfortable within your medical environment, and you may be pleasantly surprised that the facilities and skill levels are well above your expectations. This happens a lot! If you find that the medical environment is not meeting your expectations, you then can investigate alternative options.

Staying put. If you decide to give birth in Vietnam, see how your parents feel about coming to spend some time with you before and after the birth. If they are willing, you have the luxury of settling baby into its new home *and* having the support of your family *and* your local mothers group. Sounds like a win-win-win. By the way, if you want your parents to stay longer than a few days, it may be worth seeing whether it is feasible to have them stay in your apartment or whether a hotel or apartment complex nearby will give you a special deal on a longer-term stay. Also check out the visa situation for them to come and visit and how long their tourist visa would be valid.

Going home. If you decide that having the baby locally is absolutely a no-no for you, have you considered going home for a few months and then moving back? This is quite a common scenario for pregnant women but does take some preplanning. You may want to go home sooner rather than later, to make necessary arrangements and book your gynecologist or obstetrics (OB) nurse or maternity hospital. Or it may be that you have an OB locally whom you are happy with and you can just maintain email and/or phone contact with your OB back home for extra support, as needed. If you choose to deliver in your home country, your OB there will need to have your records from any medical visits you have made locally.

If you do go home, you will probably be away for around three months. Can your husband use his annual leave or organize some unpaid leave to come home with you for at least part of the time? More than likely your husband will not be able to be with you for the entire time, and you may also need to fly back afterwards on your own with a newborn—could you do that?

Key considerations. A very important point to check is which airlines will allow you to fly while in your third trimester and then book accordingly. Many will allow a woman with a "normal, low-risk pregnancy" to fly with a letter from her gynecologist or OB up until thirty-four weeks into pregnancy. Others will allow you to fly up to thirty-six to thirty-eight weeks, whereas others require you to complete your flying before you are thirty weeks.

Another key thing to check is how the location in which you choose to give birth will affect your medical coverage or insurance policy—and your personal finances.

If you do indeed "pull the plug" and go home permanently, it is not the end of the world. But a small word of warning: leaving an international assignment prematurely may hinder the chances of your husband being offered another such opportunity. It may affect your memories of international assignments, plus may cause some spoken or unspoken tension in your relationship.

We strongly suggest you think of this as a last resort option. We have seen many people go home temporarily to have a baby and we have seen many people stay on with the proviso that they return home as soon as their current assignment is complete. However, we have seen very few people (if any) leave an assignment to go home permanently for the birth of a new baby when they have not long been abroad, especially when for a company-sponsored assignment.

Ultimately there is no right or wrong answer as to what you should do. These are big decisions and ones that only you and your husband can make, once you feel informed enough to make your choice.

We wish you a happy and healthy pregnancy.

Homesick New Mother Abroad

$Q_{\textbf{\textbf{.}}}$ I am a trailing spouse and mother of one. We have been living in South Korea for seven months. When we first arrived, I loved the thrill of it all. But now I hate it. We are living in a tiny apartment with no backyard or outside space and we all sleep in the same room. My son is cooped up inside unless we take a couple of forms of public transport to get to the local park. My husband works from home on occasion, and then I have the impossible task of keeping our sixteen-month-old son quiet and occupied so as not to distract his father.

As an Australian who grew up on a large property, I had never envisaged my son's childhood or my parenting style to be anything like this. I desperately miss my mum for the emotional support and I wish she could help more with her grandson. I feel like I do not have five minutes to myself or anywhere in our home to "get away." Our situation was not like this on our first assignment in Canada. I miss Australia dreadfully and although my husband says we can go back once this assignment has finished, I have a sinking feeling that he does not want to go back to Australia at all. Can you offer any encouraging comments?

$A_{\textbf{.}}$ As is often the case for a trailing spouse, you are trying to deal with various situational, environmental, emotional and personal issues simultaneously. Ensuring that your family is safe, secure and comfortable in their new home, while you yourself are trying to figure out a new culture and navigate the emotional upheaval that this brings, can be downright difficult. Throw into the mix your new role as a parent and suddenly life looks completely different— and quite often not at all how you had pictured. More often than not, your own needs are sacrificed for those of the rest of your family unit.

Be realistic and live for today. Our first word of caution is about being too nostalgic about "home." The reality of life in your home country might not actually match your memories of "home" anymore. We tend to reflect on the positive and blank out the negative aspects of our lives, especially when we are in an unhappy space. You may be reminiscing with rose-tinted glasses on. Be careful.

Unfortunately, if you are living in the past and yearning to be back in Australia, it will be nearly impossible to adjust and assimilate in your new location. In order to integrate into or adapt to life in Korea, you need to live it and be present in it. Get out and experience new things: try new foods, go to new places, join a club, get involved in Korean cultural activities, do some sightseeing. Your life in Korea is not "instead of" your life in Australia. Think of it as "in addition to."

Positive changes you can make. Assuming that you will be in Korea for a while longer, the only real way to move forward is to articulate some positive changes that you can make in your day-to-day life that might help you to feel better about your new location. Can you change where you live? Granted, you might lose some money on the current lease, but are you able to find someone to take it over, or are you willing to lose a bit of money on the rent in an effort to improve the happiness of everyone in your home? Have you thought about contacting some estate agents to get an idea of what is available? We appreciate Korea is not the cheapest of places to rent accommodation, but you will not know if you do not investigate.

If you cannot move, can you befriend others nearby who might have an outside yard or play area, where you could visit with your son? Have you considered enrolling your son in a kindergarten or nursery for a few mornings a week? This will give your son contact with other children his age, plus space to run around and play—and it will hopefully give you the time you deserve to do something for yourself. Another idea would be to take your son out to more activities, such as swimming lessons, music classes or any other type of socialization classes that will get you both out of the apartment and feeling more involved in your community.

What about joining a playgroup (or two) of other expatriate or internationally minded mothers? This could provide you with an outlet to share your joys and struggles with like-minded new mothers who empathize with what you are going through and are probably going through the same things themselves. If there are no such groups in your immediate vicinity, you could always advertise (in local media, via a flyer at the local supermarket or via online forums) and start your own (see *Starting Your Own Club*).

Recognize realities. Another major consideration is, just how much of your frustration is due to your location versus your new role as a mother? Motherhood is a massive adjustment in itself and an ever-evolving one as your children grow. It has a huge impact on your life, given its around-the-clock responsibility, sleep deprivation and the feeling that you never have any time to yourself. These are issues that mothers all over the world deal with, so be careful not to blame these frustrations on your host country.

With regards to not having your parents around to help out, again a word of caution: many an expat has been lured home by the promise of free babysitting from grandparents, only to find that the busy schedules of grandparents today might not match those of their children. With sixty being the new fifty and fifty being the new forty, grandparents today are more than likely still working (at least part-time), regularly traveling for pleasure and/ or just being very busy in their own right.

Take action to find happiness. We suggest that once things are clearer in your mind, in terms of why you are frustrated, what you can change and what you cannot, talk to your husband (because open and ongoing communication is vital) and then set yourself some goals and time frames for making positive changes to improve your situation. If you find that you have genuinely tried to be happy in Korea but cannot, then again, you need to speak with your husband and articulate clearly how you feel and why. Together, you need to work out what is important and how you can both be happy.

Many relationships have broken up overseas (and at home) because couples cannot see how to change a current, unhappy situation. However, many other relationships have survived because together, couples have made difficult decisions (such as moving home, quitting a job and/or changing a career path) that have ultimately improved their family's happiness and kept them together.

Note: Do not be afraid to get external counseling to help both of you think about and talk through what you are seeking to improve in your current situation.

Unfortunately, not all expat assignments work out. Nor do all marriages. But before you think about separating or moving home, think how you personally, and you as a couple, can try to transform your situation so that your time in Korea might later become a wonderful memory.

Best wishes.

International Adoption

Q. My husband and I have been expatriates for some years now, living across four different continents and seeing almost everything that we feel we need to see. We are now ready to have a family and are seriously thinking about adopting abroad, from our current base in Asia.

Can you please share your thoughts on international adoption and what implications there might be for an adopted child who proceeds to grow up outside of their original country and culture?

A. First, it is important to acknowledge that the topic of adoption is *very complex*. If you have any doubts about this, just watch *Mother and Child*—the heart-wrenching 2010 film starring Naomi Watts, Samuel L. Jackson, Annette Bening, Jimmy Smits and Kerry Washington. A box of tissues later, you will likely agree that there is a huge amount to learn and consider about adoption—far more than we could possibly cover in this short response—and that adoption is an extremely personal experience for all involved that can differ remarkably from case to case. That said, here are some general thoughts to guide you.

Paperwork and procedures. International adoption can sometimes feel like an insurmountable feat—with seemingly endless paperwork, wait times, and legal and logistical requirements.

Each country—the home country and the country you wish to adopt from—will have their own set of procedures and processes that needs to be adhered to in order to complete the adoption process, so it is advisable to check with local government representatives and check online to find the exact information required.

If you are interested in adopting, be prepared to provide numerous official documents (witnessed and notarized), specific personal identification such as fingerprints, passport photos, various certificates, family finance details, and even very intimate details about the activities and beliefs of you and your current family members. Also be prepared that it might be a very expensive process, especially if you need to travel to and from a different country and potentially accommodate yourself, often unexpectedly, in that country for lengthy periods of time during the adoption process.

If you need help, there are plenty of adoption agencies that can help you navigate and/or facilitate the international adoption process. These agencies can be expensive as well, but their costs may be worth every cent to you in the long run, so try to think long term. Just be sure to consult a reputable agency—ask around for referrals, ask government departments if they have lists of accredited agencies, do as much research online about each agency as you can, and ask for them to explain all of their costs up front.

When you are deciding which country you might adopt from, you should know that the Hague Convention on Inter-country Adoption is an international adoption agreement between participating countries on best adoption procedures. For this reason, some people feel a greater level of "reassurance" from adopting from one of the seventy-five member countries.

Emotional considerations. What is your motivation to adopt? There are many reasons for adopting—and each of these will have different implications on both the adoptive parents and on the adopted child. Some of the more common reasons include:

∗ Parents may choose to adopt because they cannot have children of their own (namely due to infertility issues, or because the parents are in a same-sex relationship).

✻ Parents have lost a biological child and cannot face pregnancy and childbirth again.

✻ Parents want to give a child a "better life"—this can be a common reason for expatriate parents who adopt from the country in which they are living abroad.

✻ Parents want to raise a child, but without adding to the population.

✻ A situation has arisen in the extended family of one of the parents whereby someone in the family now needs to adopt the family member.

Infertility issues. If you are thinking of adoption due to reasons of infertility, it is critical that you and your partner first deal with the genuine and sometimes overpowering grief that follows the infertility process—a process which may have stretched over many years and may have included stressful and costly infertility treatments.

Adoptive parents owe it to themselves and to any children they adopt to come to terms with the issues raised by infertility before they pursue adoption. They both need to be one hundred percent sure they want to adopt—and shed the view that adoption is a second-best option.

Many adoption agencies will preach this as well—insisting that parents work through their issues of infertility grief first, then come back to adopt later. Ultimately, this can mean laying the dream of having a biological child to rest, which can understandably be a very, very painful admission.

An adopted child's perspective. Even if a child feels or believes that being adopted is the best thing that ever happened to them, it is important to be aware that there are a lot of emotions an adopted child may go through, either now or in the future.

Adopted children *can* adapt and adjust well into their new family, with time, patience and a lot of love and attention. In the first two years of life, children are normally building a sense of trust through their attachments to the adults who love and care for them. When that does not happen (as is often the case in orphanages), it can take longer for the adopted child to establish that sense of trust and reciprocal unconditional love—much to the anguish and hurt of their new parents—but it *can* happen.

Once old enough to understand, adoptees (either as children, or later as adults) may experience recurring feelings of loss, rejection and abandonment by their birth parents. They may wonder why they were placed for adoption or what was "wrong" with them that caused their birth parents to give them up. So, grief can also be a common emotion for adoptees. Unfortunately for adoptees, if their adoptive family is generally a happy one, the adoptee may also experience guilt for their feelings of grief—so they can be doubly tormented.

Along with grief and guilt, an adoptee may react to their experience of loss through feelings of anger, numbness, depression, anxiety or fear. These feelings may occur anytime in life, but especially during emotionally charged milestones such as marriage, the birth of a child, or the death of a parent. Note also that adoptees that experience feelings of loss or abandonment during adulthood may or may not recognize a connection between their current feelings and their old feelings about the initial loss of their birth parents.

Those adopted may also have identity and self-esteem issues, especially prevalent as they reach adolescence. Questions about their biological family, why they were placed for adoption, what became of the birth parents, whether the adolescent resembles the birth parents in looks or in other characteristics, and where the adolescent "belongs" in terms of education, social class, culture and peer group can also confuse an already-questioning teenager. The question of the influence of nature (inherited traits) versus nurture (acquired traits) may become very real to the adopted adolescent, who is trying to determine the impact of all of these influences on their own identity—trying to make sense of it all.

As always, if you or your adopted children need to talk with a professional about any issues that either of you are experiencing, we encourage you to be bold enough to do so.

International adoption. Adopting a child from another country usually means that the adoptive family will become a transracial or a cross-cultural family. We read once that studies have found that transracially adopted children appear to handle adoption identity issues better than most because they cannot pretend to be like everyone else. But again, the adoption experience varies from person to person, so this is not always the case.

Transracially adopted children tend to identify with their adopted parents' race more than their own. In order therefore for an adopted child to develop a broader sense of their identity and heritage (and perhaps greater self-esteem and pride), it is usually recommended that parents incorporate elements of the adopted child's original culture into their day-to-day life, including friendships with people of the child's ethnicity, food, and traditions. For parents, do not be scared to do this, because embracing another culture can actually be one of the unanticipated joys of intercountry adoption.

A joyous experience. Parenting brings with it both a unique set of challenges and a unique experience of joy. Parenting an internationally adopted child is no exception to this rule.

If adoption really is for you and your partner, we encourage you to talk to families who *have* adopted abroad, so that you can be reassured that it *is* possible to find treasure at the end of the sometimes arduous and exhausting adoption journey.

We wish you both all the very best—whichever decision you take.

Raising Bilingual Children

Q. Our family is British and about to move to Brazil. One of my major concerns about our move is that none of us speak Portuguese. I worry about how our children (aged four and seven) will cope. Other people have told me that children are fast learners when it comes to language and it will all work out once I get there, but will it?

I have no idea how to raise bilingual children and I question how much time I should invest in raising them bilingually, when they might forget it all when we leave Brazil anyway. Can you please offer some wisdom from your experience?

A. Learning a second language is indeed a source of concern for many families raising children abroad. Although many parents would like their children to speak another language, anxious parents may question their children's ability to learn a new language, worry about feelings of isolation and fear how their children will cope in a bilingual environment.

These concerns are exacerbated if your family has been relocated to a foreign-speaking country without any preparation or support and—as is often the case for children—without a choice. All of these concerns are valid.

Love and support. As a parent, you need to provide plenty of love and support to your children in the early stages as they come to terms with their new environment. Encouraging them to learn the language is a great way to help them adapt and feel part of the larger community. If you choose to learn the language also, it can be a great bonding experience for the entire family.

Yes, initially your children might feel a little isolated and mix up their words; that is very common in the beginning, but it does not usually last. Young children such as yours are generally very flexible and fast learners—they will probably pick up Portuguese quicker than you expect. Teenagers sometimes struggle a bit more, especially if they resent being forced to learn a new language, but again with your love, patience and support, they too should learn quickly. With a little persistence, your children's vocabulary will increase, and so too should their confidence, ability, sense of inclusion and their happiness in their new host country.

Lasting benefits of language learning. To motivate you and your children, consider these positive reasons to learn Portuguese:

∗ Your children could become fluent in Portuguese and carry this skill with them for life. According to *Wikipedia*, more than two hundred and sixty million people speak Portuguese, making it the fifth most spoken language in the world.

∗ Even if your children later lose the ability to speak Portuguese, they should still retain the skills to learn a language; the different sounds, word order, stress, rhythm, intonation and grammatical structures of any additional language are easier to learn once you have studied at least one second language.

∗ Language is a window into another culture. By learning the language, your children may gain a better appreciation of other cultures and people—becoming more globally aware citizens.

∗ Some say that multilingual skills can translate indirectly into improved analytical, social and academic skills.

∗ Speaking another language can help your children feel at ease in different environments, especially when others are speaking different languages.

* Multilingual skills can be considered advantageous for university and job applications, even if the language is not required for the position—because language skills can demonstrate flexibility on the part of the applicant.

Providing opportunities. In terms of how to raise a child bilingually, Barbara Zurer Pearson, PhD, author of *Raising a Bilingual Child*, talks about the importance of opportunity and motive when learning a new language. So first off, what opportunities can you provide to help your children learn Portuguese, both before you move and once you are in Brazil? Before leaving home, you might want to consider looking for a fun Portuguese language tutor. Ideally, for young children such as yours, find a tutor who meaningfully interacts and engages with the children—includes lots of play and creativity in their activities, and encourages independence in learning. You may also like to learn with them.

Once you are in Brazil, try to organize play dates with local children, learn to sing songs in Portuguese, and get some Portuguese movie DVDs your children might enjoy. Try to find other ways for them to interact in the Portuguese language, such as art or sport classes or other activities they might be interested in. The more interaction, the faster they (and you) will learn. However, do be sensitive if they are a little apprehensive at first and do not push them into doing something they are reluctant to do. This will only make them less willing to learn and participate.

Some expats who really want their children immersed in a new language will send their children to a local school over an English-speaking school. Language immersion is the fastest way to pick up a language, but again, be sensitive to your children's needs and think about the short- and long-term effects of this strategy.

Motivating your children. Next, think about how to motivate your children to learn Portuguese. Children must develop their own reasons to want to learn and use a second (or third) language. Do they want to learn it so they can interact with people they like or love? Do they want to watch and talk about popular television programs with other children at school? Would they like to go to the movies with their friends? Learning a new language needs to feel real and be useful—and for children, it also helps if it is a source of fun.

For older children, explain the upcoming changes and talk about the opportunity to learn Portuguese. Let them get used to the idea, rather than forcing the idea on them suddenly. If you give them time to absorb the concept and encourage them to see the advantages of learning more than one language, this might help their motivation and willingness to learn.

Investing time. In relation to your question about how much time you should invest in raising your children bilingually, Pearson says that it is difficult to give parents a number of hours per day or week. However, she did find that children who heard the second language less than twenty percent of the time (roughly sixteen or so hours per week) would understand and learn new words, but they did not necessarily start conversations or make sentences in it. So if you want your children to become bilingual, consider exposing them to Portuguese for more than sixteen hours per week.

Interestingly, Pearson does not consider someone who speaks a second language for day-to-day formal situations like schooling and classes "bilingual." She defines a bilingual person as someone who chooses to use their new language for relationships and real-life communications. So in your situation, maybe the goal is not for your children to become bilingual, but for them to speak enough Portuguese to adapt to and enjoy living in Brazil.

All in all, encouraging your children to learn Portuguese might be a fabulous investment. Be positive, be proactive, but also be sensitive—you might need to adapt your strategy along the way once you see how your children are responding to life and a new language in Brazil.

Boa sorte and all the best!

Special Needs Children

Q. We are considering taking on an expatriate posting in Central America. Nothing has been offered yet, but we are keen to try to make something happen within the next year or so. My question is about special needs education. We have two young children: our four-year-old has dyslexia and the youngest, two and a half, has just been diagnosed with autism. I am torn with guilt over wanting to go abroad and possibly thereby jeopardizing our children's education. Is it unrealistic for us to consider an expat posting at this time?

A. You are not alone in your concerns. According to the Brookfield Global Relocation Services' *Global Relocation Trends 2010 Survey Report*, eighty-three percent of respondents said family concerns remain the most overwhelming reason for assignment refusal, so you are right to pause and consider your family's needs before embarking on an adventure abroad.

Interestingly, the same Brookfield report (but in 2009) said that "every child moving to another country, leaving friends, family, his or her comfort zone in curriculum, interests, and perhaps even language of instruction, inherently has special needs"—albeit at a different level to your own children's needs.

When you move abroad, you *and* your children need to start over: make new friends; get used to a new home, neighborhood, school and country; learn a new language; and adjust to new cultural codes. If you can do this, your children's diagnoses alone need not rule out the possibility of a positive expatriate experience.

Inevitably there will be some difficult experiences in any family's move abroad, but here are some pointers to help make your potential move as successful as possible.

Be thorough in your research. Certainly you will need to do a lot of research and be as prepared as you can be, as should all families embarking on an overseas assignment. You must thoroughly research which resources and facilities are available in your target country—and, if possible, reach out to people already using those services. Ideally, personally visit, check and compare those facilities yourself.

In your research, check both mainstream and alternative education options, individual teachers who work with special needs children, medical facilities, family support groups, government assistance and any other resources that might be important for the well-being of your family. If you need help to compare education options, there are companies with years of expertise in this area whose advice could prove priceless in any relocation decision that you make.

If one of the deciding factors in your potential move abroad is the availability of household help (such as a cleaner, nanny, special needs carer, tutor, driver, and so on), make sure you research this thoroughly, because pay rates, waiting time before your helpers can start with you (due to paperwork and other due processes), local laws and expectations can vary greatly from country to country.

Assess your own emotional stability. How reliant are you on friends and family for emotional support, mental relief and having some "time out"? How comfortable would you be without your same support network readily available? Relocation abroad with children can be difficult for any parent experiencing the chaos and uncertainty of an international move, but parents of children with special needs undoubtedly have even more to think about and juggle abroad. Are you strong enough to manage this on your own (or until you meet new friends and/or join a support group)?

Find support abroad. The nature of expatriate life often means that the expat community is very close and supportive, and you should not be on your own for too long. However, do factor in your planning that new friends abroad will most likely travel more than your support network back home, so they might not always be there for you when you need them.

There may already be support groups for families with special needs children set up either as stand-alones or through an educational facility. Find out as much as you can before arriving and join up if you can. You may even be able to sign up to attend an event as soon as you arrive. Certainly there are usually a plethora of online communities, chat rooms and forums that can provide support and information. Join some forums and learn as much as possible about living abroad and moving to your particular host country. And if you cannot find a physical support group on arrival, consider setting one up yourself. (See *Starting Your Own Club*)

Be clear about finances. Moving abroad can be financially beneficial, but it can also be an expensive venture. This may be especially true if you require professionally trained staff to help with your children's education and daily life, which may currently be subsidized in your home country. When negotiating any possible expatriate assignment, make sure you are clear with your company what they will pay for and what they will not cover. Will they pay for your housing, transport, flights home, medical insurance, schooling, special care if your children require it, and so on? If not, decide whether you can afford to go on this assignment, and how moving abroad might impact your financial situation, relationship and overall well-being.

Check medical care and insurance. Make sure you are comfortable with the level of medical care in your potential location or with the travel arrangements (and time required) to get to more suitable medical care, if need be. Ensure you think about sufficient medical and travel insurance options, including medical evacuation. Understand the terms and conditions, and particularly whether there are any restrictions on where you are moving to or any moratoriums on services available.

Also, if your children require any specific medicines, check whether these medicines (or their equivalent) are disbursed in your potential new location. If they are, check the costs, requirements and availability.

You are your children's champion. How adaptable are your children? Would they react or act up if they were moved? Are they likely to settle in to a new environment easily? Do they have friends at home that they are strongly attached to?

You are your children's first support and champion. Once you have done your research and feel confident about moving to a particular location abroad, only you will know whether this is the right thing to do at this point in time for you and your family.

Weigh carefully the pros and cons. Then follow your heart.

My Teenagers Are Not Adapting

Q. Ever since we moved to Germany last year, my children, aged sixteen and fourteen, have transformed into withdrawn, negative teens that blame me for taking them away from their friends back home. They do not listen to me, do not cooperate, lock themselves in their rooms, and tell me that they hate their new lives. Far from my image of them becoming global citizens with a love of adventure, they cannot seem to see any positives about our move abroad and only want to go back home—with or without us. I am worried that this has gone on for too long and I am not sure what to do about it.

A. For teenagers, moving countries can be tough: even tougher sometimes than it is for us adults. Teenagers do not have a reputation for being overly flexible. They build their lives around their friends and understandably do not usually respond with enthusiasm when told that a move abroad will take them away from their friends and their safe, comfortable world.

Here are some general principles for your situation.

The announcement. When the news of moving arises, parents can handle the news in several different ways. They can minimize their teenagers' feelings and tell them to stop being so dramatic. They can allow them to play on their guilt strings and manipulate their way into having everything they want. Or they can realize they are teaching them valuable life lessons in the process of moving, allow them to express their feelings, and help them to understand that there are new opportunities waiting for them.

Until teenagers have a chance to build a new support system, you are it. Bring them as close as you can to the realization that having friends both near and far is special, show them the new opportunities that are undoubtedly awaiting, and respect the way they feel, even if those feelings change by the hour. Try to make a big effort to separate your own relocation rollercoaster emotions from those of your children. Otherwise, your children could potentially feed off your ups and downs and mimic your behavior.

The importance of friends. Teenagers live in the complicated world of being almost grown up but not feeling like they have nearly enough control over their lives. Moving away is evidence of their lack of control. Yet a parent's expectation that they deal with their emotions and quickly start everything anew is evidence of how grown-up they are expected to be. They also tend to believe that distance between friends ultimately means the end of a friendship. This does not have to be true. But sadly, it can be.

Teaching teenagers through example that their friendships can still remain positive even though they are moving is a life lesson they may need a few times in their life. Life does not stay static, change is bound to happen, and, of course, people have to adjust. Once you get settled, make sure your teen has plenty of ways to access their old friends: this can mean getting an Internet connection set up, encouraging them to connect via email or Facebook, and setting up Skype (or a similar free or low-cost web telephone service that makes it easy for teens to talk to friends back home).

Signs of depression. Adolescents put a tremendous amount of time and energy into finding just the right peer groups. Once a move has been made, angst or mild depression is normal; however, severe depression is not. A little melancholy over missing friends and even a broken heart over a boyfriend or girlfriend should be expected, as well as respected. But depression is something that parents need to watch for.

Signs that a teenager is depressed can include so-called normal teenage behaviors, such as isolation, disassociation from family activities, slipping schoolwork and loss of friends, but can also include suspicious behaviors that may indicate the use of drugs or alcohol, or extreme eating (or lack of eating).

While your teenagers may not come to you and disclose their depression, some will admit to being depressed when asked. Many teenagers realize that, unlike the world twenty years ago, there is no shame in depression. When teenagers become aware of their depression, they often do go about looking for ways to feel better. Some will focus on a hobby while others will start leaving clues in regards to their emotions.

Ways to help your teens adapt. There are a host of reasons why relocation can trouble a teen. For one, teens crave predictability. During adolescence, everything is changing: their voice, clothes and their responsibilities. Against that backdrop, having a stable home and social life makes a real difference. As melodramatic as teenagers can seem, ignoring or minimizing the real difficulties that moving presents to teenagers only makes them worse.

Encourage your teenager to become involved in all facets of school life, including extracurricular activities, sports or the arts. Do not worry about overscheduling; it is better for new students to stay busy, especially at the beginning. If your new school has a buddy program for new families, this might help your teenager to build relationships and quickly settle in.

By having to adjust to an entirely new town, country, school and social scene, teens have to go through the awkward process of fitting in all over again. International schools are well aware of these transition issues and are usually able to refer you to local counselors, therapists and tutors, if needed, so do not be afraid to ask for help.

Having a good relationship with your teen is important at any time and particularly critical at a time of big changes, when it can ensure a smoother transition through ups and downs. Give them some time and space to get adjusted, and at the same time observe them carefully. It is perfectly natural for your teen to mope around and be dissatisfied in the weeks and months after moving. However, if you see any signs of poor health, depression, disruption of eating patterns, total withdrawal and/or unusually poor academic results, please consult a professional. Counselors and coaches can help both parents and teenagers overcome the challenges of life—especially during a relocation abroad.

Other options to consider. If things are still not working, there are other options. You could consider enrolling your teens in a boarding school in your home country, or even a different school in the new country, or perhaps involving extended family members like uncles or aunts. Another option is a family meeting. Discussing things with the children and making them an active part of the family unit, where their voices are genuinely heard and taken seriously by both parents, can be critical. During these meetings, the children should be encouraged to articulate exactly what bothers them and why, and work together with other family members to brainstorm solutions.

If life still does not get better, we seriously encourage you to rethink the benefits of this international assignment at this particular point in your teens' life cycle. If crunch time comes, would you rather be the family that disintegrates permanently or the family that puts a higher priority on family life.

The good news. No matter how much turmoil and angst surround the first weeks or months of an overseas move, most teenagers come to accept and even appreciate the discovery and adventure that an international move can bring to their lives. Maintaining a positive attitude, despite your (and their) frustrations, is critical because as unlikely as it may seem, teenagers usually adopt the same outlook as their parents.

By identifying and taking care of your own needs, you will help your children feel more secure. Your own happiness and contentment will help to reassure your teenagers that life in a new country will most likely turn out to be just fine—for all of you!

Teen Suicide

Q. We are currently living as expats in Hong Kong. Three weeks ago, an expat girl in my daughter's class committed suicide, and the whole school is still in shock. The school held a memorial service and her class also held their own personal tributes.

My daughter is fourteen years old and seems extremely affected by the girl's death, the finality of suicide and her suicide note, which blamed her family for moving her abroad. She has become really bitter, has stopped talking to us at home and has been seeing the school counselor. I am very worried for her well-being and want to help her more, but I have no idea how.

A. Our sincere condolences to your family, the victim's family and to the whole school community. Such a terrible tragedy. Death in general is undeniably difficult to cope with, but a suicide leaves so many unanswered questions, especially for a teenager who is still developing emotionally. You are right to be worried about your daughter's well-being. At times, teenagers can be notoriously unpredictable, as they are still emotionally immature and can find it difficult to be rational, keep balanced and express their feelings. Yet at other times, they can be, or at least appear to be, "just fine." Here are some ideas for dealing with this traumatic incident.

Understand the grief cycle. The most important thing you can do as a parent is to acknowledge your daughter's feelings and allow space for her to live through them. Once the initial shock has worn off, your daughter will likely experience a rollercoaster of emotions in what is commonly known as the grief cycle.

In the grief cycle, your daughter is likely to experience denial, anger, bargaining, depression and acceptance. She may or may not experience these emotions in this order, she may experience all of these or just one or two, and/or she may keep coming back to one feeling more often. All of these emotions are considered "normal" and they are all part of the healing process.

In addition to these emotions, your daughter might feel scared at the fragility of life, at how someone can choose to stop living, or for her own mortality—something teenagers do not often stop to think about. She may show signs of mistrust toward advice given by family members and friends. This mistrust may even extend to goodwill she receives through the various activities she participates in or the clubs she belongs to. Betrayal and guilt are common emotions experienced by those in your daughter's situation, especially by teenagers who may feel they could have interpreted their classmate's actions and words better to prevent such a tragedy.

If your daughter's friends seem to be coping better with their classmate's death than your daughter is, be aware that they too might be suffering and confused, but just not outwardly expressing their emotions. This is also normal.

Whatever you observe, you and your family need to realize that each and every one of these reactions is appropriate. Emphasize to your daughter that there is no right or wrong way to feel, and make sure all family members are aware that these behaviors and emotions are all a normal part of the grieving and healing process.

Give her space. You must give your daughter enough space to grieve at her own pace. This is key. Her school counselor should help her move forward, but try not to get impatient or rush her to "feel better." Teenagers are highly sensitive and influenced easily by significant events. It is important for your daughter to come to terms with the death, get closure and move on from it, but in her own time and on her own terms. The grieving process is very individual, especially for a teen that is still processing so many concepts in life. Her grieving time frame might not match your time frame. Be patient.

Consider your teen's support network. A teenager with an adequate support network of friends, family, religious affiliations (if applicable) and/or extracurricular activities tends to have outlets to deal with frustrations and fears. However, many teens do not believe they have a support network, and this can be especially so for teens of an expat family who frequently move around. Global nomads in this position can end up feeling disconnected and isolated from family and friends and can be at risk for suicide.

So now is a good time to ask yourself: Outside of this family, who is in my daughter's support network? If you are struggling to come up with names, consider reorganizing your own schedule for a while so you can "be there" for your daughter a bit more during this rough period—even if it means just "hanging around" the home when she does not feel like talking. Plus consider very gently encouraging your daughter to join some new clubs or activities and to go out more with her friends.

Be aware, however, that there is a fine line between being supportive and being overbearing, between granting her some space and being too distant—especially given the unpredictable mood swings of adolescence. Parenting can indeed be a challenge, and you need to make the call when and how much to be there for her, and when to step back and give her some breathing and grieving space.

Maintain honest and open communication. Try to keep the lines of communication open with your daughter, and be sure to convey your genuine concern, support and love. If your teen confides in you, show that you take her concerns and anxieties seriously. Above all do not belittle what your teen is going through. This could only increase her sense of hopelessness.

If you have recently relocated, it may be that you are one of the only people with whom your daughter can honestly vent her feelings. If this is so, think about other people (your own friends, neighbors or colleagues, for example) whom you could ask to "be available" to your daughter, in case she wanted to open up to them instead or as well. Expatriate life can be very lonely and isolating at times, for us adults as well as our children—especially ones trying to cope with pain and trauma.

It is also important to talk about and remember the former classmate with your daughter. Do not minimize your daughter's uncertainties and apprehensions by glossing over the girl's death like it never happened or erasing the girl from your daughter's life. This is a pivotal moment in her life thus far, and so it is important to acknowledge what happened and talk about it freely as and when your daughter wants to.

Keep a loving eye on your daughter. Give your daughter and your family time to heal, but also keep a vigilant eye on your teen. Take any threats or talk of self-harm seriously. You may want to ask your daughter outright if she has had or is having thoughts of harming herself or killing herself.

Sometimes, teens that attempt or commit suicide have given some type of warning to their loved ones ahead of time. This does not mean that parents can always prevent a suicide, but it is important for parents to know the warning signs so that children who might be suicidal can potentially get the help they need. Do not be afraid to enlist additional professional help if you feel your daughter is struggling to accept the death of her classmate.

It may also be beneficial for you yourself to meet with a professional counselor, to help you cope and get some ideas on how to pass on coping mechanisms in your home. You may want to meet with your daughter's teachers as well, to find out how she is doing in class. Unexpectedly poor grades, for example, may signal that your teen is withdrawing at school, as a result of her friend's suicide. In this case, more proactive intervention may be necessary to help your daughter come to terms with the loss of her classmate.

Suicide is a horrible experience for everyone involved and undoubtedly will leave a permanent imprint on you all. Be there for your daughter. Listen to her. Encourage her. That is likely what she wants and needs from you right now.

Finally, remember to trust in the strength of your mother-daughter relationship. If you show your daughter that you love her unconditionally and have faith in her, over time, she will likely show you the same love and faith in return. Be positive. Be patient.

My Kids Are My All

Q. Hello. I am a lawyer who gave up my own very successful practice to move abroad with my husband fourteen years ago. We have three children, now fourteen, twelve and eleven, and we currently live in Norway. My husband travels extensively for work, and I am worried that I am too attached to my children. A close friend recently pointed out to me that my days revolve around my kids entirely and I willingly turn down social functions with adults, in case my children need me.

I am also concerned that my children rely on me for every little bump in the road and have become too dependent on me as well. They have not made so many friends this year and are constantly asking for my help, which I am only too happy to give. I have read about "enmeshed families" and how children are left without a sense of self and outward mission, and I am scared that I am robbing my children of valuable life skills in an attempt to fill a void in my own life. Any suggestions?

A. The most difficult part of resolving an issue is realizing that you have one, and it sounds as if you are on the right track with your reasoning and self-diagnosis. However, be careful not to be too drastic in your thinking: "enmeshed families" are families that tend to operate as a group rather than as individuals—independence is discouraged and even seen as disloyal to the family unit. Are you sure this accurately describes your situation?

Allow us to address your two fundamental issues: How do you help yourself to grow and develop as a wife, mother and individual? And how do you help your children grow and develop as individuals and become self-sufficient adults? Here are some points to consider.

Decide what you want from your life. What are your priorities? Give yourself some definitions to work toward—define who you are and who you want to reestablish yourself as. You have been a successful lawyer, a supportive wife and a loving, giving mother. Now what? Write down your ideal picture of your own identity, and then brainstorm how you can start to become more of the person you would like to be. Do not feel guilty about what has passed. Focus only on the "new you." If you feel stifled at home, go away for the weekend. Enjoy some downtime with no family responsibilities, and think through exactly what it is that you would like to create in your "new" life. Having your husband spend quality time with the children one weekend, without you around, is also a positive thing and might actually be a rare treat for all of you. Maybe when you come back you can plan some more "date nights" with your husband too.

Talk to your children about their priorities. Are they sacrificing activities that they enjoy because they feel obligated to be with you? Do your children feel free to express their goals and objectives? Maybe you have cultivated such a fabulous relationship with your children that you know their priorities and there are no changes needed here. But it does not hurt to ask—and give your children the freedom to respond openly.

Establish some goals. Write down your goals and the action tasks that you need to achieve these goals. At the same time, ask your children their goals and write down how you can support (but not dominate) your children to achieve their objectives too. These goals and tasks can be as significant or as small as you like. The important part of the process is allowing everyone in the family to speak up about what is important to them and checking that each family member is creating their most satisfying life possible.

Set definite boundaries. Be clear about your responsibilities and those of your partner and children. Although sometimes it is difficult to give your children the space and responsibility they need to grow and to make mistakes, it is necessary to do so for them to develop the skills and confidence they need in life. A healthy family is one in which each member can be themselves and be loved, within the safety of defined limits. Children especially need clear-cut intellectual, emotional and physical parameters, so they understand where their responsibilities start and where yours as a parent end.

Part of the experience of growing up is learning right from wrong and learning from experience, so you are quite right in inferring that your children need to make mistakes and learn from them, rather than have you catch them before they fall. This does not mean you love them any less.

Model the type of person you want your children to become. This means that if you want your children to socialize, be active, care about things and eat healthily, you need to do the same. It does not mean that they will become you, but they will notice your positive habits—and if such habits help you become happier, they will notice this too.

If new hobbies or interests mean that you are unable to pick them up from school on occasion, great. This teaches your children that you have commitments too and that they will be perfectly fine if someone else collects them, or (given their ages) if they walk or catch the bus home sometimes, or wait for you in the school library until you can collect them later. Once you stand on your own, as your own person, your children will most likely look to their mother as a role model and emulate your positive, independent behavior.

Break old habits. If you are not happy with your habits now, you need to have the courage to break them. For example, if you try to solve all of your children's problems—stop. If you try to compensate for their lack of school friends by morphing into a school-like buddy, do not—your children need to nurture school friendships of their own. If you encourage your children to skip team sports to join in family activities, change this—team sports are important in teaching your children about leadership, teamwork and adaptability in social settings. If you feel too busy with your children's after-school activities to join that tennis group you have always wanted to join, adjust your thinking. Your needs are important too, and your children are old enough to understand this, and to respect and cope with any changes you as their mother agree to make.

Give your children the freedom to soar. Above all else, believe in yourself and believe in your children. Take a step back from your strong involvement for a while and observe what happens. You might be surprised. Taking more time out for yourself might not only strengthen your inner spirit, but also be a welcome break for your children, who need your involvement but need their own space, identity and friends too.

Good luck!

Empty Nest

Q. I started the expat circuit a little later in life, at fifty-two, and we have been living in Spain for a little over eight months. I was employed back in the U.K. as a secretary for a medical clinic, and while I was not career-driven, I was motivated and occupied all the same. We have four children who have been my pride, joy and focus for the past thirty years. Our two eldest children are married and live in the next village (in England), and the younger two are still in university. When we decided to move to Spain we organized for the kids to board at their university and they seem quite happy about this—it is me who is struggling. I miss my children dreadfully and do not know what to fill my days with now that they are not with me.

I have been back to the U.K. four times in the past eight months, and each time it gets harder and harder to leave. I know I should not torture myself with visiting the kids, but it is all I can do to stop myself from crying endlessly.

It has also come to my attention that after thirty-five years of marriage and in the absence of the children, my husband and I have very little in common now—in fact, we can go out for dinner and it feels as if we have nothing to say to each other. Please help.

A. First of all we must commend you for taking such a gallant leap and moving abroad. It is a wonderful opportunity for you and something that will, if given the chance, enhance your life and give you stories to tell for years to come. Without the 24/7 responsibility of dependent children, you are now somewhat footloose and fancy-free to travel and enjoy your new life. This is a fabulous position to be in, and potentially the envy of all your friends.

However, given that you confess to crying instead of rejoicing, let us consider the following issues: empty nest sadness, visiting home, loss of your identity, and your marital relationship now that your children have left home.

Understanding your empty-nest sadness. The *empty nest* is a recognized stage in the human life cycle. It refers to a general feeling of loneliness that parents may feel when one or more of their children leave home or, in your case, when you and your children leave home (separately). It is natural for a parent to feel some sadness when their children have come out from underneath their wings, and it is quite normal to cry now and again. Do not be ashamed of your feelings—they are natural. Give yourself time to grieve and get used to what your new life looks like. Talk to a counselor (back home, in your new location, or elsewhere via phone) about how you are feeling. Communicating your feelings will help make the situation tangible for you, and once it is tangible, you will find you are able to more rationally deal with the issues at hand.

Visiting home. Beware that too many visits "home" will make it more difficult to adapt to your new situation and environment. To counteract this, plan an annual family get-together for a special occasion—for example, Christmas, Hanukah, Deepavali, Idul Fitri, Thanksgiving, a christening, birthday or Mother's Day—something you can focus your attention on and look forward to. Keeping busy will also help to abate the feelings of loneliness. Occupying yourself with this project and hopefully others in your new local community will also help you to settle and make your new location feel more like home to you now.

In terms of practical solutions, make a plan with your children to communicate regularly via phone, the Internet and email. Set up regular times to speak to your family, or organize a time for a family conference call. Webcams are perfect for this type of thing.

Losing your identity. Empty-nest syndrome is not just about "losing" your children. It can be a time when you feel confused about who you are, now that your "mother" label is less relevant on a day-to-day basis. Missing the involvement in your family's everyday activities can result in a feeling of loss of worthiness and can lead to a temporary identity crisis.

Add this to the identity crisis you are most likely experiencing in becoming a financially dependent trailing spouse, in a completely new and unfamiliar environment abroad, and it is perfectly understandable that you are asking, "Who am I?"

However, this is where you have a choice. You can either continue to feel worthless and sad, or you can make the most of your new situation by getting back in touch with who you are, to build up your confidence and start planning to really make something of your newfound freedom. Join some of the expat clubs, talk through your emotions with other empty nesters abroad, take language lessons, learn Spanish cooking, take up painting, register for an online course, entertain friends, travel—the world is your oyster!

Attending to your marriage. Unfortunately, your children leaving home can expose existing flaws in your relationship, as well as create new flaws as your personalities change as well. Being aware of what is different and how that makes you feel is an important step in avoiding the negative impact the empty-nest syndrome can have on your marriage. Readjustment back into being a couple takes some time, and the awkwardness of this is often a common side effect of empty nest. So, before you jump to any conclusion about the state of your marriage, take a step back and try to gain some perspective.

Good communication and preparation for this phase of your marriage is the key to success. Take advantage of the time the two of you have alone to talk about what could create problems in your marriage, what could be a challenge to deal with and what might bring you happiness. Sit down together and make a list of some hobbies you can do as a couple. Get out there and have some fun. There is nothing like a little Spanish dancing to reignite the passion. Your husband could be feeling upset about the same things you are, but he might just be handling his feelings in a very different way. Talk to him. Enlist a counselor to facilitate a discussion, if you need to.

Speaking of which, if you personally feel that your useful life has ended, you are crying excessively and/or you are so sad you do not want to socialize, please seek professional help. A few sessions with a professional counselor may just help you gain the clarity and confidence you need to turn your life and the direction of your marriage around.

Your empty-nest years may feel daunting, but try to think of them as a new era of opportunity in your life. Be courageous and make this era one of your best ever!

Chapter 4

Relationships

My Trailing Man

Q. I moved to the Netherlands fourteen months ago for my career. I was offered a once-in-a-lifetime job and my partner agreed that it was just too good for me to refuse, so he happily supported our move and came as my "trailing spouse." Having worked for twenty years already, my husband assured me that while he would possibly seek out work opportunities upon arrival, he saw this as the perfect opportunity for him to take some time out of the rat race and explore his interests of golf, photography and medieval castles.

The problem is, he seems to have exhausted his interests in nonwork pursuits and now keeps complaining to me that he hates it here because he is a "nobody." I confess that I do not fully appreciate what he is going through, but I know I need to do something. But what?

A. First, congratulations on your amazing job opportunity. We hope it turns out to be as incredible as you envisaged and that your time abroad strengthens your skills for whatever you do in the future. Second, you are smart to seek out ideas on how to help your partner. Some expats never do this, in favor of conveniently ignoring the problem, and unfortunately those relationships are often the ones that falter first.

Your partner's commitment. This is a common issue for all trailing spouses—male and female—especially in what originally appear to be the "good" locations. The spouse initially agrees to the adventure but then finds it does not live up to their expectations. They then shift their perspective and change their minds about just how much they are willing to sacrifice in terms of their own identity and career, in order to support their partner's.

To be fair, no one can ever really know what a situation will be like until they have been in it. A new mother can never appreciate what it is like to have a baby that refuses to sleep at night until they have one. A widower can never understand just how lonely life can be until after they have lost their life companion forever. So too, a trailing spouse can never appreciate what their new reality will be like until they are living the role, day in, day out. Take heart that if your partner's commitment was there originally, you do have a partner who is actively willing to make sacrifices to be with you. Remember that.

Ways you can help your partner. In the case of your partner, you have two choices: hold him to his commitment, regardless; or recognize that life is not as he thought it would be, and help him to figure out "where to from here." If you are committed to a successful relationship, the latter option is really your only option. Let us look at five simple things you can do to help your partner.

* *Ask him exactly what he hates and why he hates it.* Encourage him to treat the problem as he would treat a project for a business—identify and write down each issue to clarify the problem. This should not only articulate his thoughts for you to better understand his concerns, but also give you both a starting point for exploring possible solutions.

* *Help him to build his identity.* It is critical that trailing spouses feel a strong sense of their own identity abroad. If your partner does not have his own business cards, encourage him to get some made. They may simply state his name and details, or they may portray him as a freelancer or consultant of some sort. Either way, they should help introduce him at business functions that he attends with or without you—and give him a stronger sense of his identity in social settings. Encourage him also to practice

an "elevator speech" with you to describe what he does—and make sure you can deliver the same speech for him. In terms of business contacts, do you have contacts in your networks that could utilize his skills either in a paid or a voluntary sense, doing something that would satisfy him and/or make him feel useful?

* *Does he have his own transport?* For example, if you have a car, but he relies on public transport, helping him purchase a car could boost his sense of identity and freedom dramatically.

* *Help him find some other male trailing spouses.* You may not have time to join in on the local expat coffee mornings or monthly gatherings to find like-minded men for him, but if anyone is likely to find working executive women who might have male trailing spouses, it is you—so try it. Also keep your ears open at business functions for people with whom your husband might share a connection or interest.

* *Spend more time with him.* No doubt you are a super-busy executive who can never find enough hours in the day, but whatever you do, do not fall into the trap of working so much that it is to the detriment of what you would consider an important relationship in your life. A lonely trailing spouse can become a negative trailing spouse. All partners need to feel valued, useful and worthy of your time. Reorganize your work tasks, get up an hour earlier, return your partner's phone messages as soon as possible, keep your laptop and cellphone turned off on weekends if you can—and try to do whatever it takes to hold on to the things that are important to you.

Working together. You had the support of a willing partner when you began this adventure. Perhaps if you genuinely invest some time in and show compassion for your partner's situation, and the two of you make a mutual effort to more effectively communicate your concerns, your partner's support and enthusiasm should be able to be reignited so that you can both go on to enjoy your expat experience.

Best wishes to both of you!

Special thanks to Jeff Porter—a trailing man and the owner of the Ausmerican Blog (www.ausmerica.com/blog/) for his input on the original website version of this confession.

Intercultural Couple

Q. Recently I moved from my home in Denmark to live with my partner in his home country, Japan. We had been living together in a committed relationship for more than one year and had seriously discussed marriage and children, but we agreed to go to Japan together first, for my partner's new three-year job contract, then return to Denmark to settle down.

However, since we moved to Japan four and half months ago, our relationship has been having problems. It seems that the man I fell in love with in Denmark has transformed into a stranger in Japan. He acts differently, he dresses differently, and I feel he treats me with less love and respect than before. I am not working here and feel completely disempowered by the whole situation. Can you help?

A. Moving to a partner's home country can be a very daunting experience, and we applaud your courage to try something new in a place that must hold so much history and so many expectations for your Japanese partner.

If you are indecisive about whether to stay in Japan and stay committed to your partner, try some of the following tips to first overcome your feeling of disempowerment and hopefully ease the discomfort of culture shock.

Learn the language. Do you speak Japanese? If not, we recommend you sign up for an intensive language course as soon as possible. Learning the language will give you insight into Japanese culture, help you better understand the behavior of Japanese people and make day-to-day communication much easier. Language skills will also be invaluable if you plan to work in the future; in the meantime, learning Japanese should provide you with a greater sense of purpose and learning. It could also help you to better understand your partner and where he is coming from.

Get involved. Participation can give you a feeling of belonging and accomplishment. Anything you do to participate in your local or expatriate community, make friends, join hobby classes, and increase your language skills should be a positive step forward in your integration. Finding expats in your same situation can also be a real lifesaver, so cut down on your time talking to friends and family back home, and get out there and build yourself a great support network in Japan.

Employment opportunities. The loss of a professional life upon expatriation can have a profound impact on your identity and can manifest itself in symptoms similar to culture shock, such as lack of confidence, control and independence. These feelings, while difficult to adjust to, are completely normal.

If you would like to work, find out if it is legally possible for you to work in Japan and speak to as many people as you can about doing so. Spend your time gathering information about the employment situation in Japan and what cultural requirements or differences there may be between applying for a job back home versus applying for a job in Japan. It may not be possible or suitable for you to pursue a job in your profession, so you may need to come to terms with this and take the opportunity to try something new. Is there a hobby or interest you would really like to spend time developing, in the hope that this could be your new source of income? If yes, be courageous and give your new idea a go!

Impact on your relationship. Countless variables will impact your relationship when moving abroad. However, these differences will certainly come as a shock, especially after living together in harmony in Denmark. Different cultures have very different expectations and boundaries pertaining to gender, values and beliefs. Your partner's role, job and traditional expectations of him might make him behave differently toward you when you are in his home country. When he was living abroad, he had to adjust to a foreign culture, your culture, and was not bound by his own cultural norms. This information is not intended to belittle your feelings in any way, but it is something you need to be aware of: the power of cultural expectations and conformity are important, particularly in a conservative society like Japan's.

You may also need to take into consideration that your partner may be experiencing reentry shock. He is most likely busy reestablishing himself in his own culture, career and corporate culture. He may choose to spend more time at work to accomplish that goal, or he may be required to do so by his new boss. He may also feel guilty for moving you abroad, away from your established career in Denmark. He may respond defensively when you attempt to tell him what you are feeling. Alternatively, he may not even ask how you are doing because he might not want to know the answer for fear of your response.

Whatever the case, it is important to keep the lines of communication open between the two of you. As you transition into your new life, talk to your partner about your feelings and expectations for your relationship. Ask him about his feelings and try to find out the answers to difficult questions, such as whether he sees your relationship as long-term anymore.

You need to be understanding of his culture and what that means for him, but he needs to be equally aware and supportive of being part of yours. If you decide to build a life together, why not try to create your own culture that combines Japanese and Danish traditions, food, language, expectations, holidays, and so on?

Have a backup plan. No matter how in love you are, there are numerous hurdles any relationship will face. Regardless of culture or location, not all relationships survive for the long haul, so it is important to have a backup plan. Should the partnership not work out, you will need a plan to get back on your feet financially and emotionally.

Try to keep your job skills current or work on developing new skills to increase your value in the marketplace. If you can legally work in Japan, try to work, even if not in your chosen field—so you will have some degree of financial independence and you will also have some new experience to add to your résumé.

Be open to possibilities. Finally, be open to new experiences and be ready to face the unexpected. You are living a great adventure and learning valuable life lessons. Use your time abroad as a chance to decide on and create the kind of life that you want and deserve.

One way or the other, you will grow to become a stronger person from this experience. Make your decisions carefully and believe in yourself. You will get through this.

He Wants to Go Home

. . . .

Q. My boyfriend and I both moved to Belgium for work just over a year ago. I am really enjoying my job and I love living here, but my boyfriend does not. He has been stressed with his job, homesick and depressed, and he has finally decided that he needs to go back home. I am now in a dilemma about what I should do. I love him and cannot imagine being here without him, but maybe the timing of our relationship is not right, because I feel that living abroad is my opportunity of a lifetime and I do not want to leave. What should I do? Could we make a long-distance relationship work?

A. We feel for you in your predicament. You most likely already know that there is no right or easy answer to this situation, and therefore it is difficult for an outsider to tell you what to do. If you look deep inside your heart, we hope you will instinctively know the best road to take. To help you with your decision-making, here are some factors to consider.

Your options. The first issue to address is whether your boyfriend would consider any other alternatives to moving home. Would he consider trying a new job in Belgium or studying? Or could he capitalize on this time to travel around Europe, using Belgium as his home base so you can continue to have regular contact and meet-ups? Think about what you like about living in Belgium and what your boyfriend does not like. Is there a place that could combine what he likes and what you like? If so, would you both be willing to move there together?

Your big decision. You are in a position that does indeed require a big decision, and so we strongly suggest you take all the time you need to work through your thoughts to make the decision that is right for you. Needless to say, emotions are running high, and they can certainly sway your rational thinking. If possible, do some soul-searching: take some time away from your job, your home and your boyfriend to sit down, reflect and think hard about what you really want.

It sounds as if you are committed to making the most of your time abroad and have already invested a significant amount of time and effort into making a positive, satisfying life for yourself in Belgium. We suggest you be hesitant about hastily resigning from your job until you are really sure of what you want to do and where you want to go. A premature decision could lead to resentment toward your boyfriend if you find yourself unhappy or disappointed that you quit your job or left Belgium too early. Your job is probably also your financial lifeline, so do not cut your lifeline until you are sure you have another.

In terms of helping you to reach a decision, writing can be an excellent way of sorting through your ideas, capturing your thoughts and unraveling how you are feeling. Perhaps start a couple of lists based on each scenario. For example:

Staying in Belgium. What are the pros and cons if you stay? What are your anxieties and concerns about staying on in Belgium on your own? Do you consider that giving up your job would be a sacrifice that you might later regret? What about losing your boyfriend: could you live without him and how would you feel if he never came back?

Going home. What are your worries about returning home with your boyfriend? What would you do if you repatriated? Are there other factors in the relationship that need healing and might not heal automatically just because you repatriate? Could any cracks in your relationship get worse if you repatriate? If so, how would you cope with a breakup at home and what would you do then?

Try to be honest, impartial and true to yourself. If there are any demons in your relationship, it is better to face these sooner rather than later. Be sensitive to your boyfriend's needs and emotions, but remember that just like you, he needs to decide what is best for him. Weigh the pros and cons, as well as listen to your heart. Seek the help of a life coach if you need to, who can help you establish your life goals and offer a different perspective.

Long-distance love. Maintaining a healthy, loving relationship from a distance is never easy—especially if you and your partner are based in different locations or share the same home base but one (or both) of you travel a lot. It would be naïve to think that a long-distance relationship could meet the same needs of both partners as a relationship where you are both living permanently in the same location.

Time apart from your boyfriend may prove to you and him just how special your relationship is and enable you both to forge a deeper bond. However, be prepared that on the flip side, time apart may make you realize that you (and possibly he) are happier and more fulfilled focusing on your own needs right now.

Know that you are strong. Whatever option you choose, be aware that any decision is likely to be tough on you both in the beginning. But try to commit to a decision and give it some time to work out. If after a few months of trying, you find that it really is not working, you have already proven to yourself that you are strong enough to make one decision, so you can certainly make another. You are likely stronger than you give yourself credit for.

Keeping Secrets

Q. I am feeling a bit down because I have the sense that my husband is keeping secrets from me. He is getting more distant from me and he always seems too tired to talk. I realize that his work here in Bahrain is quite demanding, but we have been married for ten years and have lived the expatriate life ever since we got married, so long work hours and his frequent travel are normal to me but I have never felt this way before.

Maybe my mind is playing tricks on me, but all I can picture are worst-case scenarios, and my mind just seems to be going around in circles. I have tried to talk to my husband about how I am feeling, but he says that nothing is wrong and that he is not keeping anything from me. I am not convinced. What can I do?

A. We empathize with your situation and regret that it is causing you such uneasiness. We do not think it is strange that your mind is going around in circles, but we do think it is important to recognize that there is a potential problem and to reach out for help. Try to recall the moment when you first noticed your husband being more distant or tired. Try to remember the situation you were in, and see if you can find any similarities with other occasions that caused you to have this feeling. At times like this, you need to follow your honest intuition. Often your hunch proves correct—especially if you have been married for ten years. But then again, sometimes it does not.

Four areas to assess. Your situation brings up several potential areas to assess. The first is that sometimes the passage of time and changes in your life can bring with them a slow but steady growing apart in a relationship. That does not necessarily mean that this is the case in your situation, but surprisingly, when really forced to be honest, many couples who take off their rose-colored glasses will admit that after ten years of union, they are not as close to each other as they were in year one.

The second is that maybe he really is just working late and coming home too tired to connect with you in the same way that you have expected in the past. Expat assignments can genuinely involve long work hours and numerous after-work functions. Did he change roles or duties around the time that you noticed him getting more distant? Or do you think it is possible that he is starting to get a little worn down from ten years abroad and may need to take a break from the expat whirlwind for a while?

The third area to consider is you: how has being an expat wife for the past ten years affected your own sense of well-being and your expectations of your husband? Are your days filled with activities that you find satisfying, or are you feeling frustrated at various things in your life? Are your nights filled with activities you enjoy, or do you spend your time just waiting for your husband to come home—giving your mind ample opportunity to run around in circles? This may be a good time to reevaluate your own schedule and personal interests. It is never too late to take up a new study, start an exercise routine, join a new interest group, change your own work situation, or engage in another stimulating pursuit.

The fourth area to consider is that maybe your husband is keeping secrets from you. In this case, you then need to ask the how, why, when, what if, and so on. If you feel that your husband may be having an affair, work out a strategy to approach him (again) about this possibility, when he is not exhausted and when he has more time to listen to you closely. Alternatively, he may be keeping secrets but they may not be what you think. Maybe something at work is making him feel bad—for example, a missed promotion, an unsupportive team environment, a serious mistake on his part, anything that might make him retreat within himself and not feel like sharing with you his workdays as he did in the past. Or maybe he knows that he will soon be retrenched, or sent elsewhere, or something else he is not ready to talk to you about, until he is sure of his company's intentions. Or maybe it is a health issue, a financial issue, or some other kind of issue that is bothering him.

The importance of good communication. In all of these areas, communication is the key, as it is in any successful relationship. Try to keep communication open and not strained. Many factors can hinder your ability to communicate effectively with your partner. When you do manage to talk, listen to what he is trying to say. Do not interrupt or try to argue with what he is saying but just listen, just like you would like him to do for you. When your husband has had his say, summarize what he has told you. This will show that you were paying attention and understand his point, and it will help ease tension.

If you are having trouble talking to your partner or do not seem to be able to get your point across clearly, then try writing it down. Doing this gives you time to think about what you want to say and express it in a way your husband will understand and hopefully receive in a less confrontational environment. Creating good communication in a relationship can be a long, ongoing process, but it is a critical one.

Quality time together. For a healthy, happy relationship, it is critical to spend quality time together. So if your husband is too tired to communicate properly after work, maybe you can meet him for lunch on a regular basis, rather than waiting until he comes home exhausted. And maybe, just maybe, he does need to better manage his workday, so he can consider quality time with you as an important part of his daily life. It is never too late to reignite the flame and put a bit of excitement back in your relationship.

Think about something you would love to do together. Plan for it. Then do it. Then plan the next exciting event, and so on. Also think about including more physical intimacy in everyday life—even if it is just an extra hug or cuddle on the sofa.

Healing your relationship. Relationships, like all good things, require patience, effort and sometimes, healing. If your relationship does need healing, take comfort in the fact that a relationship *can* usually heal—if you both want it to and are both willing to work on it, together.

We wish you both a smooth journey forward.

Divorce Abroad

Q. My nineteen-year marriage has been slowly disintegrating over the past four years, to the point that I am now seriously considering divorce. I thought accepting our first international assignment to South America a year ago might help to rekindle our relationship, but it has done just the opposite. We argue more than ever and for all intents and purposes live separate lives. I have never felt so isolated and alone—the exact opposite of what I was hoping to achieve by us moving abroad together.

I have spoken to others about the legalities of getting a divorce here. One person told me that if I file for divorce locally I could get nothing at all, whereas if I wait until I get home to file for divorce, I would be more likely to receive at least fifty percent of our joint assets. The problem is, we still have two years remaining on my husband's contract and I am pretty sure he would not agree to us settling a divorce at home, let alone early. I am feeling so trapped and vulnerable. I cannot think what to do. Can you offer some thoughts please?

A. We regret that your marriage has come to this. Without knowing you personally, we feel we need to say up front that before ending a marriage, we highly recommend that you explore all alternative options—with the help of a professional counselor or life coach—to be sure you have exhausted all possibilities to save what you once most likely cherished. This applies even if you do decide to end the marriage, as it will help you know for sure that you tried your best before ending what has now become a twenty-year partnership.

Asking tough questions. In addition to exploring with a professional counselor or life coach the reasons why your marriage has been slowly disintegrating over the past four years, we suggest you think critically about what has made your situation worse since you have been abroad. Can you articulate a time or situation that was the catalyst for your unhappiness? How has moving away from home changed your relationship?

Have you lost some self-esteem, confidence or identity since you have moved? Or conversely, have you gained more self-esteem, confidence or a stronger sense of identity? What about your husband—how would he answer these questions?

Do you see more of your husband now, or is the problem that you see less of him because he is either always working or always socializing in the name of work? Has money affected things—and if so, how exactly? Have you felt satisfied in your work or other pursuits in South America? Do you like South America, or does it cause you stress, anxiety or discomfort?

Many, many possible factors may be contributing to your downhill spiral since you moved abroad. We suggest you explore them because you really need to figure out exactly why your relationship is now at a crisis point. You can then ascertain if there are genuinely any things you can do to improve your newfound situation—especially being so far from your previous home base. The best way to do this is to get out a pen and paper and write.

Think through every aspect of your (new) life and be as analytical as possible. Arguably, even if you know you are likely to leave your husband, you will personally benefit from knowing everything that contributed to the relationship's demise—and whether living abroad is something that you should do again. Living abroad can be a tough transition and is not for everyone. Having the courage to recognize this, if this is the case, will serve you well in the future.

Considering divorce. In terms of divorce, you need to make one or two decisions—not necessarily today, and not necessarily at the same time—and they are: (a) To file for divorce or not; and (b) where to file for divorce (if applicable).

Only you can make the first decision. We hope you do not have to make the decision alone—talk to a professional counselor first—but ultimately, *you* need to make the decision, based on what *you* personally want for the future. Define this by picturing what you want to be doing in five to ten years' time and with whom.

The second decision requires a bit of research on your part. What you heard about divorce laws in your current country may or may not be true. You need to find out for certain. Make an appointment with a reputable, locally based divorce lawyer—ideally one who has experience with expatriate divorces—and ask all of your questions. It is sometimes not a bad idea to make two appointments, with two different lawyers, to check that the information you receive is accurate. This is one area of advice where you do need to be one hundred percent correct. Your home country's consulate or embassy should be able to provide you with contact details of lawyers in a confidential manner, if you do not want to mention this in your social circles.

Improving your current situation. Finally, we can appreciate that an uncertain relationship, combined with your first international assignment, can indeed leave you feeling vulnerable and trapped. But could there be "other" more tangible issues or concerns that might be exacerbating those feelings? Do you have your own transport, or are you relying on taxis to get around—or, worse, relying on your husband's office car, when it is available? Do you have a computer and Internet access at home, so you can communicate freely with friends and family—and still feel connected to the world via news sites and other websites that reflect your passion or interests? Do you have your own bank account and/or the freedom to spend money freely? Are you able to jump on a plane, without first seeking your husband's permission, to meet up with friends back home or to explore new places of interest?

The sense of control that these simple freedoms provide can be life changing. They may or may not be enough to save a marriage, but they may well save your sanity in the interim.

There is a lot to consider, but whatever you decide, be brave and be true to yourself. We wish you all the best.

Picking Up the Pieces

Q. I am in a complete state of shock and have no idea where to turn. My husband of twenty-two years came home last night and told me he wants a divorce because he is in love with somebody else. We have been expatriates for seventeen years, have lived in seven countries and have three dependent children. I have been financially dependent on my husband for all of our expatriate years, and I have no idea how I am going to survive and make a living for myself from now on.

Gosh, if I could have seen this coming, maybe I could have planned for it in some way. Instead, my head is spinning with a million and one questions: Where am I going to live? Where are my children going to live? How will they see their father if he continues to stay here in Barbados? How am I going to support myself financially? How can I pick up the pieces and survive this nightmare?

A. We can only imagine all the thoughts and questions running through your head at this time. Divorce can be a mind-numbing and life-altering experience in itself, but there are added complications for divorce in the expatriate community. Expatriate relationships go through a myriad of unconventional stresses and strains, which can sometimes forge a deeper relationship, sometimes cause a distinct rift between the couple, and sometimes, unfortunately, lead one of the partners to be seduced by the excitement of a new person and want to end the relationship.

Practical concerns first. In addition to the overwhelming emotional and psychological strain that divorce causes, numerous practical and logistical concerns present themselves in the face of divorce overseas. We suggest your first step should be to obtain a reputable divorce lawyer who specializes in family law. It is very important not to take any action that can affect your divorce rights before seeking credible legal advice. You need to determine what your rights are, what you are entitled to, and the legal situation or requirements in your particular country. Determining these can be somewhat complicated for an expatriate and can depend on factors such as your nationality, where you were married, where you are currently living, your residency status and where you are filing for divorce. It is also advisable to employ a different lawyer than the one retained by your husband.

You may also want to meet with a professional counselor to help you sort through the questions you have and mentally process your circumstances and options. Allowing yourself to believe that you have options can be difficult at times. Considerable thought, questioning and external guidance may be necessary to help you see that you do have options and to help you sort through both these and your emotions. If nothing else, a counseling session usually proves to be a priceless sanctuary for you to voice your side of the story, without the worry of what others think in your (usually tight-knit) expat community.

Managing your finances. In terms of finances, if you have been actively involved in the household finances and investments, you will understand exactly how much money you and your husband have access to and you will know how to access some of it, in the short term at least. If you have never actively managed the household finances and investments, you are not alone. Many expatriate spouses come unstuck when they need to know what they have money-wise, where it is and how to access it. Talk to your lawyer about how to best determine your assets and liabilities, and then make a commitment to yourself that you will be more in control of your finances. For example, from now on, make sure you understand how bills are paid and have all the various passwords for phone and Internet banking as well as access to all the accounts. Keep abreast of your monthly income and especially your expenditures.

Consider your future options. To respond to your concern about how to support yourself in the future, there are two key questions to consider: How is your husband going to assist you, given the many years you invested in your relationship and raising the family; and how might you earn your own money in the future?

Many expat spouses, both male and female, who have experienced significant periods of time out of the paid workforce are understandably concerned about resuming work (at home or abroad) and presenting a conventional résumé. Self-confidence and self-esteem may also be running low and anxiety at a high, compounding the issue.

Sometimes it may be difficult to believe you have anything worthwhile to put on a résumé at all. However, think of it this way: everything you do and almost everything you experience can be translated into skills and honed for a certain job. You just need to think creatively about how to describe the attributes and skills you have nurtured and acquired on your travels.

For example, have you served on the board of a club? If so, in what capacity and what were your tasks? Would you say that you are skilled at networking across cultures, with a broad spectrum of people and job roles? Do you have an understanding and appreciation that people operate differently according to cultural boundaries and are you flexible to work with those differences?

All of these are valuable attributes that employers may be interested in, and you should make them known. Consider using a professional résumé writer in the location where you are seeking to work to increase your chances of getting "in the door." It is much easier to convince an employer of your experience and skills when you are sitting in front of them—so getting a great résumé organized is really your first and most important step, in order to secure that all-important interview.

Think about starting a business. It might also be worth exploring the idea of creating your own business (see *Starting a Business*). Being an entrepreneur usually allows you much more flexibility in terms of your work hours, especially if you become the primary caretaker of your three dependent children. You could start a business based on your new skills in the cross-cultural/ global mobility field, or perhaps use this opportunity to build a business based on one of your true hobbies or passions. When you are up to it, seek out advice, talk to other entrepreneurs, and see if there is something you would love to work on each day that could also translate into a satisfactory income.

Remember to call in favors from your friends and networks— both locally and abroad. They will most likely be only too happy to help you out in your time of need, either with emotional support, a temporary place to stay, a possible job contact, or even a financial loan. You might be amazed at what you could receive, if you swallow your pride and just ask.

A new beginning. Finally, while incredibly painful right now, be assured that the end of your marriage does not signify the end of your life—it just means the end of one chapter and the beginning of a new one.

The most important thing for you to do at present is to allow yourself time to breathe, to grieve, to talk about your emotions and to process this major shock. Eventually things will work themselves out. It may just take a little time for your new future to come into focus.

We wish you well.

Domestic Violence

Q. My friend is being beaten by her husband. She belongs to my book group here in Slovenia, and the other day she burst into tears and told me everything. Her husband is very stressed at work and apparently drinks a lot and then comes home and gets angry very easily. My friend is studying online and she is so frightened that he is going to be extremely angry if she does not get perfect marks. She had to beg him to let her take this course in the first place.

My friend's husband rarely lets her go out in the evenings because he likes her to be home when he gets in. One evening our book club ran a little late and we did not see her for two weeks after that. She told me the other day that he beat her so hard that night that she ended up in hospital for four days.

I am so worried about my friend, but I have no idea what I can do to help her. They have been married for fifteen years and I have only known her for just over a year. Is it my place to tell her to leave her husband? Are there any support networks to help her? What can I do?

A. Statistics on domestic violence are horrific. "At least one out of every three women will be beaten, coerced into sex, or otherwise abused in her lifetime," according to Amnesty International (December 2010). Sadly, these statistics do not change because a woman is living as an expatriate. In fact, expat life is arguably a scenario ripe for someone to carry out abusive acts.

How abuse happens. The foundation of domestic violence is that abusers want to dominate and control everything in order to get their own way. This can be easily achieved living away from the support and visibility of friends and family. In most expatriate families, one partner is the breadwinner and determinant of the overseas visa (usually the man), and the other is financially dependent and typically bound by more visa restrictions abroad (usually the woman). As a result, the woman can feel beholden to, guilty and obligated to her husband because he is the provider, especially if he enforces this belief. She is usually unemployed or underemployed and may have low self-worth as a result, especially if she was previously employed in a more meaningful job elsewhere. In her new country, she can feel very alone, vulnerable and financially dependent.

Unfortunately, this kind of isolation often allows the abuser the opportunity to assert and maintain absolute control. He does this without as much worry that family and long-held friends will find out—and with the knowledge that his spouse often has no one to confide in. She needs him, in order for her to stay abroad, and if children are involved, she usually feels even more trapped and dependent than in her home country.

Types of abuse. Abuse can be physical and/or emotional. It can include physical assault such as hitting, pushing, shoving, sexual abuse (unwanted or forced sexual activity) and/or stalking. Arousing fear and preventing a person from doing what they want or compelling them to behave in a way not freely chosen by them is a means of control. Although emotional, psychological and financial abuse are not regarded as criminal behavior, they are very real forms of abuse and they can lead to criminal violence.

How to help. You need to know and tell your friend that abuse is not an accident. It does not happen only because her husband is stressed at work, is drunk or has a short temper. Abuse is an intentional act that one person uses in a relationship to control the other. Make sure she understands that this is not her fault—she does not deserve this, and no one deserves to be treated this way. There are steps you and your friend can take to help ensure her safety.

Importantly, as difficult as it may be, you need to remain impartial and not get involved in family affairs. Offer emotional support, love and understanding. Assist and help her in any way you can to ensure her safety, but your friend must make any final decisions herself. You do not want to become an accomplice should her situation become a legal concern, nor do you want to compromise your own safety if her husband is angered by your involvement.

Embassies and consulates should have a list of safe places or shelters for your friend to go to. They may also be able to offer advice on getting out of the country, taking children, facilitating financial support and addressing visa or passport concerns. You may also like to research whether there are any domestic violence hotlines in your city she can call to talk to someone about her situation.

Plenty of resources are available online to offer support and advice. Be aware though that her husband may check her home computer's online activity, so searching online from your home computer or from an Internet café is perhaps the more strategic approach.

Sadly, local police may choose not to help people involved in domestic disputes abroad. However, you may want to call them on your friend's behalf and find out their policy on intervening in domestic violence cases with foreigners, then report back to your friend accordingly. If they are willing and do attend to such calls, perhaps ask your friend to warn her neighbors to call the police if they hear angry or violent noises. If the police will not help you, you know you do not have the option of calling the police and you will know not to waste precious time trying to do so. Make sure your friend has important phone numbers on her at all times, including the police (if useful), a taxi service, ambulance service, crisis hotlines, airlines, friends and her embassy or consulate.

Planning for her departure. Your friend must decide what she wants to do in terms of the future of her relationship. If she chooses to stay, then that is her prerogative and you must respect her choice. If she decides she wants to leave, you can help her to consider the following:

* *Travel documents.* Your friend needs to gather as much information about her legal rights and options as possible before making any attempts to leave. She needs to be one hundred percent sure of her rights and legal ability to leave her husband and/or leave the country with minimal risk to her person and her future. Will the embassy issue a temporary travel document if she cannot get her passport? What will this mean for her status in her host country and also when she arrives in her home country? Does leaving impact her citizenship status and/or her other legal commitments (banks, credit cards, and so on)? What are the legalities surrounding taking children away? She does not want to get to the airport only to be sent home (to an extremely angry husband) due to a legal hitch. (Often the abuser will hide passports, so it might be a good idea for her to start looking for her or her children's passports now, when her husband is not at home.)

* *Identity papers.* Your friend should gather as many legal documents (originals or copies) as she can. These could include birth certificates, medical records (especially if they make note of injuries sustained from abuse), health insurance, bank books, copies of bank statements, pension schemes, drivers' licenses, marriage certificate, work permits, copy of host country visa, any form of ID with a photo, address book, and so on.

* *Safe haven.* Counsel her to practice ways to get out of the house safely and think of a few places she could go if she left home suddenly.

* *Access to cash.* Your friend should consider opening a bank account or getting a credit card set up only in her name. This can be difficult to do in some countries if you are not working, but this may be something a family member back home could help with. At the very least she should start putting some cash aside in a safe place now, so if she needs money for an escape, she has some.

* *Getaway bag.* She should also start packing a bag of essential and everyday items (including valuable or sentimental items) that she can grab and leave with in a hurry if/when the opportunity presents itself. Make sure this is hidden in a secret place or stored at a friend's, so her husband cannot find it.

* *Extreme vigilance.* Tell your friend she needs to be aware who might be watching her, on behalf of her husband. For example, if she has a driver, it is possible that her husband quizzes her driver about all of her movements and her phone calls. For this reason, she may need to be smarter than her husband when she plans what she does each day.

Supporting your friend. We admire you for supporting your friend and we wish her a very safe and happy future.

One parting word of caution: your friend may not feel able to follow through with all of your suggestions at this point in time. Leaving is a big step and requires a lot of courage and emotional strength. Try not to take this personally. Just be there for her and support her efforts to rebuild her strength and confidence, so she is best able to protect herself and/or her children. That is what she most needs you to do.

Expat Infidelity

Q. I am currently volunteering for a telephone helpline, which is aimed at the expatriate community here in Indonesia. We have received more than one thousand calls since opening last year, and I find it disturbing that one of the main issues in our expatriate community is infidelity. I listen to the outpouring of pain in each individual case, and I read plenty of stories about expat infidelity on the Internet. I cannot help but wonder: why does infidelity seem so pronounced in expatriate communities?

A. We applaud your volunteer efforts at your local expat helpline. As you have experienced from volunteering at the helpline, expat communities can sometimes feel like magnets for mischief and infidelity—well, at least compared to life back home in suburbia. However, anyone who has ever seen the American television series *Desperate Housewives* will know that infidelity, betrayal and heartache infiltrate suburbia as well.

Infidelity is common worldwide and expatriate communities are by no means immune from the pain of marital unfaithfulness. It is worth noting too that while men are traditionally more likely to stray, women are equally capable of engaging in infidelity. Key trigger factors for infidelity include a lack of regular, quality communication in a relationship; work pressures; financial pressures; loss (of a job, friend or loved one); more-than-friendly attention from a third party; and/or the physical absence of one of the partners—perhaps due to travel or other commitments.

Added expat triggers. However, in addition to these triggers, there are added factors in the expat community, which may help to explain why you listen to so many cases of infidelity at your local expat helpline:

* *Culture shock.* Everyone reacts differently to culture shock and the consequences of being thrown into a completely different environment.

* *Loss of identity.* Leaving a purposeful role and identity at home to become a "nobody" overnight can be a very tough transitional process.

* *New, unequal distribution of power in a relationship.* One member of a couple is working (and has possibly been promoted for this international assignment) and is enjoying the "best side" of the new location. The other member is often not overly occupied and may feel isolated as a result. They may be adjusting to financial dependence and may start regretting their decision to move.

* *Loss of support networks.* Being uprooted from a stable support system at home to move abroad and start afresh is never easy.

* *Loss of accountability.* Some expats feel that being away from their family, friends and historical ties gives them the freedom to act differently abroad, without fear of social repercussions from their old networks back home.

* *King and queen mentality.* Unfortunately, with some expat packages (namely those with very high salaries, drivers and home helpers) and/or some expat jobs (where local staff can unrealistically exalt an expat's status), some expatriates fall victim to a seductive sense of invincibility.

* *Cultural differences.* Some local men and/or women lavish foreigners with excessive attention (either for genuine reasons

of admiration or for the purpose of angling for personal financial gain). This attention cannot usually be matched at home and can often forge the rift that leads one or both members of the couple to look for satisfaction outside of the marital relationship.

* *Greater spending power.* Indiscretions and other excesses can be more easily masked (at least temporarily) if expats have more financial spending power abroad.

* *Different nightlife abroad.* Most employer-sponsored expatriates have many more evening work responsibilities (such as functions, corporate events and business networking) than they did in their home country. They work hard and they often play hard, which results in greater situational opportunities for infidelity or out-of-character behavior.

High exposure. Infidelity may also feel more prevalent in expat communities simply because word gets around quickly. Despite most expats living in big cities abroad, it seems that an expat's "dirty laundry" is shared and aired among their international community in the same way it would be if they lived in a small country town. Marital separations (which often involve one or both members of a couple repatriating) can gain high visibility in local expat circles.

Types of infidelity. Regardless of location, cheating on a partner usually stems from a need. The need can be either physical or emotional, but cheating most often occurs when a person is in search of something. For example, it could be the need for attention or intimacy or, as is often the case in an expatriate setting, the perceived need for novelty in one's love life.

Cathy Meyer, a certified divorce coach, marriage educator and legal investigator, outlines five types of infidelity on About.com:[2]

[2] http://divorcesupport.about.com/od/infidelity/p/infidelity_type.htm

* *Opportunistic infidelity.* This occurs when someone is in love with their spouse but gives in to their sexual desire for another person (usually due to situational circumstances, risk-taking behavior and/or alcohol or drug use).

* *Obligatory infidelity.* This type of infidelity is based on the fear that resisting someone's sexual advances will result in their rejection and/or loss of attention.

* *Romantic infidelity.* In this situation, the cheater might be committed to their marriage but has very little emotional attachment anymore and longs for an intimate, loving connection with someone else.

* *Conflicted romantic infidelity.* This type of infidelity occurs as a result of love and sexual desire for more than one person at the same time.

* *Commemorative infidelity.* This occurs when the marital partners have no feelings for the other person (anymore), but stay together for fear of failure if they were to separate.

Preventative measures. Living abroad is challenging both for individuals and for relationships. Many books suggest that infidelity is most likely to occur in relationships where communication is limited and the individuals are under pressure. To help boost the longevity of any relationship, it is important for each member of a couple to maintain quality and plentiful communication, despite the pressures of day-to-day life.

It might be a good idea for couples to openly discuss the expat triggers outlined above and perhaps even encourage each other to identify "stop signals" each person could commit to, if they find themselves thinking of straying outside their mutually-agreed-upon rules or boundaries.

Expat families should also make a concerted effort to provide every family member (especially "trailing spouses") with the opportunity to realize their potential abroad. Continual personal growth and development is vital for the well-being of every single person and can arguably help avoid some of the factors that can lead to unhappiness in a marriage (potentially from both parties) and marital unfaithfulness.

Do not lose faith. With regards to your work at the helpline: continue to listen empathetically to your callers and support them. Encourage them to seek the help of professional marital counselors who are trained and well versed in the issues and consequences of infidelity.

Most importantly, do not lose faith in expatriate communities. They are full of genuinely wonderful and happily married people as well.

Keep up your great work!

Online Betrayal

Q. My husband has a new high-powered position in Kenya and has been there without me for three months. I know his situation has been stressful, but I believe he is relishing the challenge, the power and also the adoration he is getting from the local women working in his company. He tells me about the women that he interviews and how on one occasion the candidate said she would willingly sleep with him!

Now I discover that during my absence he is conducting online affairs with women. I accidentally discovered this and was deeply horrified to read the intimate details shared. He justifies his actions by saying that nothing physical has ever happened and that he is able to detach himself from me when conducting these online conversations. He says that he has been lonely and stressed and that this is his way of relieving boredom. Please help me decide what to do.

A. We appreciate how you must be feeling. It sounds like you have every reason to be upset. Betrayal is a very painful experience in any circumstance, and inevitably it causes us to reevaluate our relationship. Relocating to Kenya as a successful Western male is bound to attract local female attention, and your husband's authoritative position would only enhance this. He may be caught up in new feelings of power and desire at work and in his social interactions with women—who are apparently offering him admiration, adulation and a whole lot more. As a result, he is feeling flattered and his judgment may be clouded—circumstances not helped by his distance from you and all things familiar. Your husband might be in unfamiliar territory and genuinely not know how to handle the additional attention.

In the period you were not there, he turned to cybersex, where he says he can escape the stresses and strains of real life. However, he seems to have forgotten that even though you were not physically present, you were (we assume) emotionally available.

The online affair that he has been having is damaging to your relationship, even though it is not physical. When an online affair is romantic in nature and involves sharing intimate information, as you mentioned, it is difficult not to see that as an interference and intrusion into your marriage. Online dating still involves a "real life" person, and extracurricular romantic involvement in any form with an individual other than one's partner is a betrayal of trust and loyalty.

The need to talk. Ask your husband how he would feel if it were you who was conducting online affairs. Walk him through the scenario with the same intimate details he was sharing via his online liaisons. Perhaps he might benefit from someone holding up a mirror in front of him, to help him see the person he has become. He needs to understand why what he is doing is detrimental to your relationship, and he needs to take ownership of the damage he is causing. The important issue then is whether or not he is willing to change his behavior.

Face-to-face conversations are critical. In the same way that your husband claims he is able to detach himself from his online conversations, he is also likely to detach himself from his conversations with you via telephone. A face-to-face conversation will likely bring the situation more into his reality. Jump on a plane and go and talk to your husband, so he can see and feel your pain, without the convenient luxury of being able to dismiss the topic in a nightly telephone call. Your husband needs to see that online affairs can be just as damaging as offline affairs. Visiting for the weekend is not enough either: try to postpone all of your other commitments for the next few weeks and reconnect again in more of a real-life setting than just a work-free weekend.

When you talk face-to-face, share with your spouse exactly how you feel and ask him for his thoughts. Let him tell you what he feels, and try to give him some time to do this without passing judgment or getting angry. Does he feel let down and alone because for some reason you have chosen not to move to Kenya with him? Would you reconsider joining your husband, not only to be there for him but also to help save your marriage?

Make sure to let him know that you are there for him when he is feeling uncomfortable, stressed, irritated, upset, sad or lonely. If you are honest with yourself and you think you have not really been there for him lately, decide if you want to be and, if so, make sure that you are.

Decision time. Your husband then has to choose what is more important: his online affairs or your marriage. If you are both interested in keeping your marriage alive, you may want to discuss various options to make this happen, such as changing jobs and/or location (either you, him or both of you). Many expat men before him have given up lucrative jobs in an effort to salvage their relationships and to reconnect with the values they held before. It is possible.

However, there is no escaping the fact that there is now tension in your relationship. Together, you need to decide if there was tension before and whether you could both commit to healing the relationship. Do you want to be together in one, five, ten, twenty years? If yes, do not live under any illusions—now that this has happened, you will both need some time to work through these issues and feel passion for each other again.

We recommend that you look for professional help to assist you in the process of getting your relationship back on the right track. Make it a priority to spend time together and focus on each other. Think seriously about doing whatever it takes to live in the same household and in the same country again. This might involve some major sacrifices—from both of you.

Words of hope. Try not to react in haste. Talk things through. Give your marriage a fair go. These will be challenging times, but know that you *can* get through the pain and the challenges. With or without your husband—you *will* be okay.

A Lonely Affair

Q. My husband and I have been on assignment here in Bangkok, Thailand, for three and a half years. Life has been good to us— and we have always supported each other when times have been tough. However, last year, things changed. My husband's company promoted him to the role of director, Asia Pacific, which meant that our assignment was extended for another three years. I agreed to this, but was devastated because I had already made plans to restart my pediatric practice back home when our assignment was due to finish here at the end of last year. Since then my husband's new role has become very demanding and has required him to travel a lot.

Sadly, my loneliness has led to an affair with my neighbor. My neighbor is a sweet, caring and educated man who makes me feel so good about myself. I feel guilty about what I am doing because I really do love my husband and want our relationship to get back on track. Ironically, I started the affair to ease my loneliness, but now I feel lonelier than ever. What should I do?

A. Unfortunately, you are not alone. Many relationships start to come undone abroad when one person is absent from the relationship due to long work hours and/or frequent travel, and one person is left at home waiting. When someone lends an ear or shoulder and makes time for you, especially when you might be struggling, we can understand how you might go against your character and become drawn to them.

The situation becomes complicated, however, when that ear does not belong to the person to whom you are married and your emotional dependence falls more and more on the "other person." The relationship becomes a problem when you start trusting in this person more than your husband, if you find yourself turning to this person to get all of the support you need and/or if the relationship becomes romantic.

The fact that you have acknowledged there is a problem, is a step in the right direction. You have identified what you are missing in your marital relationship and stated that you want your relationship to go back to how it was. This might just prove that you have the will and strength to pull your marriage back together.

The relationship and the reasons. There are two pivotal issues we suggest you address. The first is your affair and your affection for your neighbor. As wonderful as your neighbor makes you feel, if you really want to set things right with your husband, you need to stop having your affair. This means you need to stop turning to your neighbor for emotional and/or physical support. Given your neighbor's close proximity, you also need to seriously consider confessing to your husband, because although neighborly relations will likely turn extremely sour once your husband finds out, think through the consequences of your neighbor telling your husband before you do.

The second and most important issue is to address the reasons *why* you are relying on your neighbor for support, so that it does not happen again. Marital affairs are often the visible symptoms of an underlying psychological issue that the sufferer has not come to terms with. Before you can address the actual affair, you need to try to understand the *why*.

You mentioned that you were devastated when your husband was promoted and your time in Bangkok extended. Could it be that you hold your husband personally responsible for your delay in being able to move back home to your life and subconsciously you are lashing out at him through this affair? Your husband is now all-consumed with his new, high-travel role, which has meant that you are feeling neglected and lonely. Could it be that you resent your husband and his success now because you are left home alone feeling lost and angry? Are you missing your husband's love and companionship and subconsciously looking for things to fill that gap in your life now?

Voicing your frustrations. We suggest you work through your frustrations of an extended stay in Bangkok and what that means for you. Speak to your husband about his traveling and how this makes you feel. Whether you tell him about your affair or not, you need to talk to him about how serious the rift is in your relationship. Many a husband who has said that he cannot reduce his travel schedule has later, in a relationship crisis, found that there really *are* ways to cut back on the amount of travel they need to do personally—sending delegates sometimes instead or solving problems via phone calls, videoconferencing and the like. It is amazing what high-travel executives can do when they realize that their work behavior is being destructive to their family life. Remember, your husband, like most high-travel executives, probably cares deeply about his family and would not want to seriously jeopardize his family for the sake of his job.

Rebuilding your relationship. You may both also need to become more proactive about making time together. Perhaps you need to start to schedule special date nights in his diary or join him on one of his work trips (combined with a stay over a weekend). This might help to rekindle your intimacy, and you can start to transfer your emotional dependence back onto your husband and away from your neighbor.

Although be warned: if you confess your affair to your husband, he might not be so keen on date nights in the short term. Being told that your partner has had an affair can take months if not years to mentally reconcile, as a huge element of trust has been broken and trust is not repaired easily.

Rebuilding your inner strength. Start to look at ways to rebuild your inner strength, confidence and resilience, so that you are not unexpectedly turning to others for support when your husband is away. Reconnect with the organizations, friends and contacts you were connected to during the first three years when you were happy in Bangkok. Alternatively, join some new clubs, take up a new hobby or start a business (see *Starting a Business*). Keeping busy with something that is meaningful and significant to you will offer much-needed distraction and help build your confidence again.

Very few people become successful without a team of supporters behind them. Treat yourself as important and rally a team to support you in your mission to revive your marriage. This might involve seeing a psychologist, who is trained to work through issues like this with you in a professional way.

A life coach might also help to re-inspire and motivate you personally, helping you to articulate your values and set goals for yourself, along with supporting you and keeping you accountable in your efforts to achieve the things you really want in life.

A better life. Accept responsibility for your actions, work through your pain, and if you tell your husband, be willing to support him through his pain. Then focus on creating a better life for you, your husband and your marriage.

It will be a tough journey, but you can do it.

Chapter 5
Mixed Emotions

Overcoming Negativity

Q. I am becoming increasingly negative and pessimistic and cannot help but be cynical and contemptuous toward everyone and about almost everything. This is my second posting overseas with my husband, and I know I am becoming more and more impossible to be around. I find myself uncontrollably ranting negatively about everything here in Israel. I used to be such a relaxed and pleasant person to be around, but now I am spiraling out of control and I have no idea how to return to my usual self. Can you help?

A. According to the Brookfield Global Relocation Services' *Global Relocation Trends 2010 Survey Report*, sixty-five percent of employer-sponsored expatriates who fail to complete their assignments, cite spouse or partner dissatisfaction as the primary factor. This means that you are not alone in your feelings, and we hope you will not be too hard on yourself.

Choose associates with care. As to why you have become cynical, your response may stem from a general feeling of loss of control—a very typical experience for expat partners. It may also have to do with the people you are associating with. A trailing spouse once told us about her first luncheon with an international women's group in a new posting. She had been in town four days and was very enthusiastic about being there and meeting some people. The first question she received upon arrival was "What did you do to deserve this?" followed closely by "How long is your sentence?" No surprise, she came away very demoralized. She subsequently decided that this particular group of women was not for her. She did not want to associate with or be surrounded by such overt negativity.

Watch your reaction to problems. If you are not particularly "busy" in your new life, it is very easy to spend your unoccupied time focusing on all the things that go wrong. This is true of life in general but is exacerbated in expat life because of the unfamiliarity of everyday living and the different challenges you face abroad.

For example, an Internet connection problem in your home country may be just a matter of over-the-phone technical support to very quickly solve the problem. By contrast, an Internet connection problem in a foreign country, with a foreign language, may involve several attempts to get someone to help, and may not be fixed for days, if not weeks. In the meantime, the nonfunctioning Internet connection means it is not as easy to connect with friends and family at home. It also means you are cut off from easy access to virtual services that expats rely on, such as banking, world news, travel, education and more.

Challenges like this can send any rational, self-controlled person into emotional despair. Unfortunately, they can also incorrectly feed your mind with thoughts that everything is wrong with your current location.

Nothing will change the situation you are in, but you can change your reaction to each situation. That is something you do have control over.

Environmental triggers. The environment can have an impact on your mood too. Have a look at your daily routine, take note of what really annoys you, and modify your actions accordingly. If it is being pushed and shoved by crowds of people on the streets when you do your shopping, look for alternative places to shop or try to change the time of day you visit the shops or market. Perhaps check whether the major shops offer delivery services, so you can avoid the crowds altogether. If it is the heat and humidity that pushes your buttons, try to plan a holiday away during the worst weather and/or do your outside chores in the early morning or in the late evening, to avoid the intense local heat. If you are not the coffee-morning type, look for different associations or networking groups that you can join to associate with like-minded people instead.

Equally, take note of the things that make you feel good and put you in a positive frame of mind, and do more of those things! Exercise can be one of the main saviors for people suffering from negative and depressing thoughts. That is because exercise stimulates the release of endorphins and makes you feel happier. If you do not do so already, try incorporating exercise into your daily routine. Make being active a priority and focus on improving *you*.

Investing in your health. Finally, do not be afraid to get help if you need it. There is no shame in investing in a life coach, doctor, professional counselor, psychiatrist or other medical specialist to help you get through patches in your life where some external moral support and direction could be beneficial.

In particular, if you are finding that your feelings of extreme negativity have been going on for several weeks and you are losing interest in your hobbies, friends, family and everything around you, it is possible you may be suffering from depression. In this case, we urge you to seek professional help sooner rather than later. Turning to a professional could genuinely be one of the wisest investments you will ever make in yourself and in your relationships with your family and friends.

We believe that (perhaps with some help) you *can* turn your expat experience around into a much more positive one. Make sure you believe it too.

Medical Treatment Abroad

Q. I am an expat living in China who has been diagnosed with breast cancer. I am very sick and am undergoing chemotherapy in one of the international hospitals here. The hospital and care seem adequate, but I feel uncomfortable because not all of the medical personnel speak English—and on top of that, my first language is French. I am wondering whether I should stay here or move back to France.

Separating the family is not an option for us, so moving back would mean that my husband would have to find another job and we would have to take the kids out of school early. I am torn—on one hand I want to be in a familiar environment with French doctors, but on the other hand I wonder whether the medical care at home is really any better than what I am receiving here, which my friends assure me is genuinely first-class. My family is very supportive, but can you offer some independent thoughts?

A. We are very sorry to hear of your cancer diagnosis. Cancer is such a devastating phenomenon and it is very unfair—for both the sufferer and their family.

Feeling safe. Our initial instinct in times of uncertainty is to make ourselves, and those we love, feel as safe and secure as possible. This would explain your concern for your family and your idea to return to France for your medical treatment. Being in a familiar environment, with a common language and surrounded by a familiar support system, helps make everyone feel safe and could also give you a much-needed sense of control over what is happening to you.

However, for expatriates, the choice of where to go for significant medical treatment is never easy. Should you trust the local system? Should you travel home for treatment, even if it involves uprooting your family? Here are some considerations to help guide your decision-making.

Medical treatment abroad. Unless you have been a resident in your country for quite a while, it is likely that the environment (and most certainly the medical system) is foreign to you. Language and cultural differences can also alienate. However, it sounds as if you have the loving support of your family and friends in China and you have already been receiving treatment in a quality international hospital, so perhaps some of the unfamiliarity has passed and just the language barrier and general uncertainty about your condition remain.

Have you looked into options to help overcome the language barrier? Many of the large international hospitals abroad have translators working either as consultants or as full-time staff. If they do not offer this and cannot source a quality translator for you, perhaps you know someone who could go with you to the hospital and translate? Or perhaps you could pay an independent (English- or French-speaking) interpreter, to accompany you on each hospital visit? The cost of doing so is likely to be quite minimal—especially in the big scheme of things.

Medical treatment back home. You may also wish to contact your medical provider in France and ask if they would be available to speak with you about your condition, if you felt you needed clarification on any aspects of your treatment abroad. A second opinion is often very reassuring.

Another idea is to find current or former cancer patients that could share with you their experiences of being treated for breast cancer in France. Go online and research breast cancer treatment in France or join French forums discussing breast cancer. Sometimes our nostalgia paints an unrealistic picture of what things are really like back home, so it could be beneficial to have an up-to-date and realistic view of medical care in France before making any critical decisions.

Following on from this, instead of relocating your whole family to France in the first instance, think about returning by yourself (or with a friend) for a short visit to try cancer treatment back in France, so you can more accurately compare it to your treatment experience in China.

Cultural differences. Differences between cultures can extend into the health care system, revealing themselves in such things as doctors' bedside manners, the medical and emotional treatment of patients, and physicians' attitudes toward their patients and staff.

For example, in some cultures, physicians can be very autocratic and authoritarian, making patient-doctor communication difficult. The doctor caring for you may not want to discuss your condition in detail with you or be readily available to answer questions you may have. This does not necessarily mean your care is substandard. Your doctor may be doing an excellent job of diagnosing and treating your condition; they just might not be very communicative with you.

Emotional aspect. In addition to your level of comfort with the local hospital system, you need to consider your emotional needs. Moving back to France is a tough decision, because as you know, it will cause significant upheaval for your family. However, your family likely only want what is best for you, so if you believe returning to France will create an environment that is more conducive for your healing, then moving back to France could be the best decision you could ever make.

We suggest you make a list of advantages and disadvantages for each scenario and talk through your thoughts with your family. Take into consideration how your cancer will be treated, how long your treatment and recovery are estimated to be, and how comfortable you will be in either place. The medical staff may have some advice for taking care of yourself after chemotherapy, and these lifestyle changes may need to be reflected in your home environment. The prognosis you receive from your doctor will play a vital role in your decision and in your recovery, so seeking a second opinion from your French doctor might be helpful.

Physical considerations. Another aspect to ponder is your support system. Do you feel this would be stronger in China or in France? If you enjoy domestic help in China, will you be able to enjoy similar help to make your day-to-day life easier back in France? Or instead will you have extended family to lend you a hand with cooking, cleaning and looking after your home? If you returned to France, could your partner take some leave from work to care for you if you become very ill? If you are taking the children out of school in China, can you find appropriate school places for them back in France?

Medical insurance. The issue of medical insurance cannot be overlooked. Will your insurance policy cover long-term treatment for you both at home and/or abroad? If finances are a concern, the answer to this could also affect your decision.

There is no simple answer to whether you should stay in China or return to France temporarily or permanently. Try to gather as much information as you can about your physical condition and prognosis. Speak with medical staff in both countries, and speak with your immediate family about the options of staying or moving home. Make a plan and then focus your energy back where you need it most—on you and your health!

Best wishes for your return to full health.

Holiday Sadness

Q. I am working in Dubai with my accompanying husband and three daughters. We have been here for almost eight months, and so far so good. However, Christmas is coming up and I have just been told that I will not be able to have time off work to return home to the United States for the holiday season, because Christmas is not recognized as a holiday here.

Unfortunately, both of our families back in the United States (as well as my husband and children) have taken the news very unfavorably. I have tried to explain the situation to everyone, but given that our families are extremely close, always spend holidays together and have a strong belief in continuing traditions, I know that they feel it is my fault for "ruining" their Christmas holidays— and now even I have found myself thinking this way. I feel so guilty. My contract is for three years so we have several more holiday periods to go. How should I handle this?

A. Balancing work and family responsibilities never ceases to be a juggling act—and holiday periods are no exception. Working mothers are typically torn between work commitments, expectations from extended family and the role of the nurturing female figure at home. Expat mothers also have cultural differences or restrictions and oceans between family members thrown into the mix. On the positive side, there are some steps you could take to try to appease your families.

Step 1: Address family issues. We will start with your immediate family. Is your husband on your side? Does he understand your predicament and support you? Standing together on an issue such as "deciding" to not go to the United States for Christmas will demonstrate to your children that these are family decisions and that you support each other. It will also take the blame directly off your shoulders. Having said that, is it an option that your husband and children go back for the Christmas break? We realize that you would not want to be separated from your husband and children at Christmas time, but if you find that going back to the U.S. is super important to them, perhaps some compromise could be sought in terms of the holiday periods important to you as a family. Alternatively, is paying for some key friends or family members to visit your family in Dubai an option? Try to think creatively, and try to think what you would do for the holidays if you were the nonworking partner in Dubai?

Step 2: Keep traditions alive. Just because you are currently living in a country where your customs are not recognized does not mean that you and your family should be deprived of them. Make a point of keeping up traditions that are important to your family, your religion and your ethnic background. Keeping important traditions alive will also help children feel connected to their culture and help strengthen their identity.

A child growing up as a third culture kid (TCK) can experience an extreme sense of confusion as to what belongs to them and what they belong to. In new environments, it is important to provide a sense of stability and security, so try to continue celebrating certain occasions as you would in your home country. Maybe ask your parents to send over Easter eggs if you cannot buy them, improvise your Thanksgiving dinner if you cannot find a turkey, and make your own Christmas tree if need be. It is not how things are done that matters, it is that you are continuing the familiar that is important. Also, try to take at least one annual leave day for at least Christmas Day, so you and your family can still *feel* like it is Christmas at your new home in Dubai.

Step 3: Make some reasonable suggestions. As for your family back home, do they really feel you have single-handedly ruined Christmas, or do *you* feel you are responsible for ruining their Christmas? Either way, everyone needs to be reasonable. This does not ease your guilt, but they of all people should understand your situation. We assume that they, like you, consider your family to be close, so they should know that those feelings have not changed just because you are not physically there. Do you have a webcam? Arrange for an online videoconferencing date with your family and open presents together or do something else that is really fun. Perhaps you could suggest a family Christmas in Dubai next year. Better still, what about an all-family holiday in a fun and exotic location (maybe halfway between Dubai and the U.S.) in January or February instead?

Step 4: Create positive experiences. If you are still feeling guilty about "depriving your children" this Christmas because they are without their grandparents, take a step back and refocus on all the exciting opportunities you are exposing them to abroad instead. Your children will only see Dubai as a place full of exciting opportunity if their parents and role models believe as much—so take the lead and model some of that excitement! Lead by positive example and your children will follow.

We know some families who have had to improvise when celebrating their own traditions abroad. Now that they are back home, years later those improvisations have become part of their family traditions. Try to think positively and create experiences that may likewise become part of your family's ongoing Christmas traditions.

Happy holidays. Try to stop feeling guilty. Ask your family to help you think creatively about how to spend this holiday season and what to plan for future holiday seasons. Then work together as a family unit to enjoy yourselves!

I Think I Am an Alcoholic

Q. I live in Athens, Greece, and I think I am an alcoholic. I am spending more and more nights drinking. I find myself choosing unimportant evening social functions (through my job here) over getting home and spending time with my family. I will literally spend a few hours on Monday morning planning my evening functions for the week, based primarily on which function will be serving the most alcohol and which function is likely to last the longest. This situation has been going on for some time now, but because of my position in the community, I have never felt comfortable or anonymous enough to ask anyone for help.

Last weekend, I had a huge argument with my husband. He accused me of being an alcoholic and he threatened to take our children and move home. I am beside myself and shocked at how it has come to this. Before this posting I had never been a big drinker, and in fact I counseled two women in our previous posting who were drinking to cover up a miserable marriage. How could I be so blind as to not see that this interest in socializing is what is happening to me? I could really use some help right now.

A. We appreciate how difficult it must have been for you to write this. So often we become so involved in the day-to-day running of our lives (and our family's) that we do not have the time or inclination to look up and notice what is going on around us or to us. As accomplished, capable and intelligent women, the "truth" can come as quite a shock.

Getting the support you need. If your drinking is starting to interfere with your family life and your husband is the one pointing this out to you, then you have an obligation to your husband and children to do something about it. The place you need to start is with professional help—either Alcoholics Anonymous or "AA" (which has an active chapter in Athens) or a private therapist. Or for best results, both.

Understanding why you drink. People turn to alcohol for many different reasons, and not all alcoholics have similar symptoms. Some people find that only alcohol can make them feel self-confident and at ease. They get addicted to the "buzz" that alcohol and the social environment gives them and may think about occasions to drink constantly. Other people turn to alcohol to escape something in their lives, such as stress at work, an unhappy relationship, family responsibilities, painful memories, financial worries, illness, feelings of guilt, homesickness, or a multitude of other reasons.

Being truthful about your habits. Without them always knowing it, drinking (and its side effects) typically start to take over an alcoholic's life. Not only is the period of consumption of concern; the next day many alcoholics experience extreme guilt and fear— especially if they became drunk without planning to and cannot remember what they said or did the night before.

Alcoholics often sneak drinks, lie about their drinking, hide bottles, drink at work, drink at unusual times (such as in the morning), drink alone, or make up excuses to find ways to drink. This affects their general demeanor, plus it affects the trust and honesty in their relationships as well as the trust and honesty they have with themselves. This in turn leads to even more feelings of guilt and shame—often making them feel out of control and unable to stop their patterns.

Do any of these situations apply to you? If so, or if you are not sure, joining a fellowship such as AA will help you get the support and find the strength you need to quit drinking. Support and/or counseling can help you to recover before your health becomes a major concern and while you still have both your job and the love and support of your family. It is never too late or too early to seek support and get help for any type of addiction-related illness.

If you are now at a stage where you can acknowledge that you are possibly an alcoholic and you want to do something about it, pat yourself on the back. With a commitment to positive action, you are about to turn your life around.

Finding support for your family. There are also two support groups for family members of alcoholics: Al Anon and Alateen (for teenagers). These groups provide understanding, strength and hope to anyone whose life is or has been affected by someone else's drinking. Both of these groups may be helpful for your husband and your children, to enable them to get support and understand what you are going through. This can be a very scary and doubtful time in a relationship, so hearing the experiences of others who have been through it and successfully came out the other end can offer much-needed clarity and hope—for everyone involved.

Seeking professional help. We also suggest you employ the expertise of a professional counselor. Alcoholism is usually an outlet to "numb" feelings associated with other areas of your life. Whatever the issue, you owe it to yourself and your family to seek professional help. A professional counselor should be able to help you get to the root of the problem—determine why you rely on alcohol—and help you get past this.

Keeping positive. You and your family are in pain right now. But be positive: you *will* overcome this—especially if you open up and let your family in to help you.

Believe in yourself, and believe in your family who love you.

Adult TCK

Q. I am an adult third culture kid (TCK). I have spent my life in Papua New Guinea, China, Turkey, the United States, New Zealand and now the Middle East. Of these places, New Zealand, my passport country, is always the most difficult location for me and I have only ever lived there in short bursts. I find it difficult to fit in, to feel accepted, and to understand the millions of rules both written and unwritten. I think it is easier to just stay abroad. Will I ever be happy in my passport country?

A. Take heart: the doubts that you have are quite common among TCKs, characterized as a feeling of not knowing where you belong, especially when you are spending time in a passport country that feels anything but familiar. Because you have been brought up in several cultures, you may feel no real ownership in any one country or culture—and being "home" may make you feel more of an outsider than ever, especially if your day-to-day interactions do not involve other like-minded TCKs or repatriates who can share your experiences and give you a sense of "community" at your home base.

Being an outsider at home. Every culture has millions of rules, both written and unwritten.

The good news for expats is that when it is obvious you are a foreigner, no one is expecting you to be "the same" and you are generally excused when you make mistakes in a social context. In their passport country, however, TCKs (and adult TCKs) generally physically look and sound like others in the dominant culture around them, so when they "mess up" a cultural rule, they may not be as easily excused as would be someone in the same situation who more obviously had come from a different place. Hence use of the terms "global nomads" and "hidden immigrants" to sometimes describe third culture kids.

Where do TCKs belong? Most TCKs build relationships with all of the cultures in which they have lived, while not having full ownership of any. The good news, however, is that while you may not feel you completely belong in your passport country, there is a place that you do belong. Because culture is something shared, not an individualistic thing, the "third culture" is actually a place where its members historically experience the commonalities of a cross-cultural lifestyle, high mobility and expected repatriation at some point. TCKs commonly feel a sense of belonging more in relationship to others of a similar background than to a particular culture or country. In other words, regardless of nationality, TCKs (like many other subcultures) tend to have more in common with one another than they do with the general population in any place that they have lived.

If you do not already, we strongly encourage you to maintain as many links with your TCK friends as possible. These days, with the help of the Internet and especially blogs (which tend to allow for very open and honest expressions of how people are feeling in their everyday lives), connecting with other (adult) TCKs is arguably easier than ever. A growing number of online resources are available to help TCKs transition "home," stay connected and feel a sense of "community." Seek out these resources and proactively get involved.

Choosing to stay abroad. Another great way to stay connected with like-minded people is to continue to work abroad. You seem to have chosen a career that allows you to live overseas, which is great. This can also help TCKs like yourself to feel like they "belong" somewhere—the "somewhere" being "within a group of expatriates," rather than in a particular country.

Deciding where is "home." Maybe another question to ask yourself is, where do you want to live? If after much effort you decide that you really do feel out of place in your passport country, do you really need to live there?

Basically, your home is the world; it is not related to a geographical location per se. The saying "Home is where the heart is" would apply to some degree in your situation. Because of your varied experiences, you can see life in terms greater than one cultural boundary and can explain and express yourself in more than one culture. Your fears of never being able to fit into your passport country might be accurate, but then again, you chose a career that allows you to travel and live overseas, so why not keep living the life that you have enjoyed leading so far?

Adjustment is possible. If you do decide to live or settle in your current passport country, your transcultural identity and flexible mind will help you to cope. Find other TCKs who live in your home country and connect with them. Share your feelings and you might be amazed at how many others are out there facing the same issues. Start your own (adult) TCK or repatriate network; others have found this process to be very cathartic and empowering—you might too.

Meeting new friends. Connecting with TCKs is important, but remember that there are many non-TCKs out there also waiting for your hand in friendship. You have some unique skills and some great advantages coming from your global past, so by all means use them—in whatever you do and with whomever you meet.

The world offers globally minded (adult) TCKs like you a *tremendous* host of possibilities. Go forth and enjoy!

Special thanks to Ruth Van Reken (www.crossculturalkid.org), co-author of the authoritative Third Culture Kids: Growing Up Among Worlds, *for providing valuable input on the original website version of this confession.*

Friends Back Home

Q. I am living a fabulous expat life in Asia, but I am missing the camaraderie I once enjoyed with my friends back home. I try to share stories of all the amazing things I am discovering abroad, but I feel my friends are jealous and do not want to listen. Other times, I want to confide in them about the guilt I feel over living so far away from our aging parents, or about how my children are struggling to fit into school, or confess the loneliness I experience during my husband's travels, but when I try to voice anything about my expat life, my friends cut off the conversation and are not interested.

I miss being able to share my ups and downs with my friends back home and I feel resentful that I have to hide details about my life abroad. I am worried that my expat life will ruin my long-held friendships. Any tips?

A. Maintaining friendships while abroad involves time, effort and sensitivity. Of course you want to be able to share your experiences and happenings with your friends back home. Your life has taken on new excitement and each day is novel, challenging and stimulating, so you have a lot of stories to tell and a lot of enthusiasm to share. Your whole way of life is different—you probably have a new social circle full of well-traveled people from all over the world, maybe you are traveling more for fun weekend getaways to discover new places, you might have time now to follow one of your passions, and you may even be enjoying the time-saving benefits of a household helper or driver.

However, that is a whole lot of change for anyone to comprehend—especially someone who is not living the change.

Consider the realities. Remember, while your life has taken on new meaning and is full of excitement, your friends' lives back home may not have changed much at all. They are probably still in their routine: they go to the same hangouts, visit the same sports clubs, endure the same traffic headaches and go to their same job every day. They might feel like they have nothing interesting to share with you and it is easy to see how some resentment can build on both sides.

Both parties need to be realistic about this. And perhaps you need to ask yourself: Would I be jealous if I were the one stuck at home, when my friend was abroad, living the "good life"? Trying to put yourself in your friends' shoes might help you to understand how to relate to them, now that your social circles, travel itinerary and interests have changed.

The question is just how jealous or envious they are, and how it might affect your long-term friendship. Unfortunately some people are unable to overcome this, so contact dwindles and the friendship dissipates. You might need to be prepared for this worst-case scenario.

But on a more positive note, there are certainly some tips that we would recommend in order to help maintain a healthy and positive relationship with your friends back home.

Keeping in touch. Our first suggestion would be to make sure your friends back home realize how valuable and important their friendship is to you. It is always more difficult to be the one left behind and their envy is natural.

Regular contact is vital, and with the Internet, this should not be too difficult. Emails do not have to be long-winded novels detailing every occurrence in your daily life, but a quick note to let your friends know you are thinking about them should help nurture a relationship and ease any jealous feelings. Low- or no-cost Internet-based telecommunication providers such as Vonage and Skype are also a great way to keep in touch.

Try to plan trips back home as often as you can and make sure you spend quality time with your friends. This can be difficult when time is short and meetings with the bank manager, financial advisor, real estate agent and dentist can get in the way, but try to make time. Doing this reinforces how important these people are to you, and face-to-face contact will rekindle the relationship. Also encourage them to visit you, if they can, as this will make them feel part of your life, see your frustrations first-hand, and make them appreciate the ease of getting things done at home. Plus, it will be a wonderful experience that you can reminisce about in the future.

Sharing common experiences. In terms of hiding your life, try not to think of it like that. Instead, try to think of it as being able to share part of your life with your friends back home and part of your life with your new friends abroad. Focus on sharing with your friends back home some of the daily pleasures, difficulties and/or frustrations you might have both at home and in your new location—so that your friends can relate to the issues—rather than talking about your household helper, driver or multiple holiday travel plans.

Your friends might also find it difficult to relate to some of the location-specific frustrations you might feel. Select the stories your friends back home would most want to hear, just as they are probably doing when they are communicating with you.

True friendships. If you are serious about wanting to sustain these friendships, then you will *find* a way to stay in touch and stay excited by each other's conversations.

So, be proactive and help make these friendships last a lifetime!

Retiring Abroad

Q. I have always dreamed of retiring abroad to live by the beach in the Caribbean. So now, at the ripe young age of fifty-five, I am seriously contemplating living out my dream. I should be bursting with happiness, but instead, I find myself overwhelmed with anxiety and worry about whether I am making the right decision. I am scared about making new friends and sad about giving up the ones I will leave behind. I am tossing financial figures around in my head all day, checking that I will have enough to cover the cost of living in my new location. Can you help?

A. Retiring overseas can be an exciting lifestyle choice. However, making sure that it is the right decision for you depends on countless factors, ranging from legal issues and practical concerns to cultural differences and emotional upheaval. The only way to help alleviate your concerns and ensure a positive experience is to do your research. Make sure you have all the facts and know what you are getting yourself into. Here is an initial checklist to help.

Investigate legalities. First and foremost, are you legally able to retire to the country of your choice? Many countries around the world have opened their doors to retirees and offer a number of programs to make it easy for retirees to settle in their country. But some have not. Go online and/or speak to your local consulate or representative of your intended retirement destination to get up-to-date information and find out all of your options for legally moving to your country of choice.

In many cases, qualifying for a retirement visa is as simple as presenting proof that you have sufficient funds from your home country to support yourself abroad. But be aware that the local laws of many countries may prevent you from working or engaging in any gainful activity, so this also needs to be factored into your financial viability assessment. In addition, be prepared to undertake a health exam, vaccinations, a criminal background check and/or some rigorous paperwork requirements to meet immigration criteria. Again, research as much as possible before you make a final decision.

Research financial implications. Your financial state of affairs is really your ticket to a successful overseas retirement, so it pays to make sure your finances are all in order. We highly recommend that you hire a reputable financial advisor (or two: one in your home country and one in your destination country), to help explain the implication of taxes, inflation, interest rates, bank accounts and cash flow, and so on in both places.

Are you able to claim a pension from your home country? Will this be transferred to your overseas bank account and easily accessible in your new home? What about currency and exchange rates? Again, make sure you are very clear about how any transfer of funds will work. It is extremely important to ensure you have cash readily available.

Be wary of hunting down "expat retirement tax havens" to make your home. While on paper these can obviously seem very attractive options, make sure you genuinely want to live in one of these countries, regardless of the tax benefits.

Part of the financial research process should include a check into the cost of living for foreigners in your destination country. Cost-of-living surveys are done by a range of fee-for-service companies, but snippets of their results can usually be found in various publications online. Remember too that the cost of living for a local might not be the same as for an expatriate—depending on your expectations for food, clothing, accommodation, services, and so on. You should also factor in flights home (for both visits and emergencies) into your budget, as well as travel you may want to do in and around your new home country.

Consider medical insurance. Another very important aspect is medical insurance (which is often a requirement for a retirement visa) and the accessibility of high-quality health care. Make a point of researching the medical facilities in your intended location and whether you would even be entitled to use the local health care system. Make sure you are familiar with the ins and outs of your medical insurance and what exactly it will cover. Read the fine print and speak to a customer service advisor before you purchase a plan. Be aware that your current medical insurance policy may not cover you if you live abroad, and some local medical policies in your new country may not cover expatriates.

Think about family separation. Another important factor to consider is your ability to live away from your family. Although you can access technology that will enable you to keep in contact relatively easily (for example, Skype, Vonage, email, webcams, and so on), family separation issues are a leading cause of premature repatriation and should be considered prior to retirement abroad.

For example, does the thought of watching your grandchildren, friends and extended family over the computer, and not in person, cause you heartache? Think carefully whether you will be able to sacrifice less physical contact with those you care about to live out your dream of retiring abroad. Or, if you plan to visit often, prepare for that both emotionally and financially.

How will you adapt abroad? When you have the practical issues taken care of, take some time to focus on how day-to-day life will look in your new country. In addition to the various cultural differences and potential language issues, keep in mind your destination country's level of development, quality of life, bureaucracy, stability, accessibility and security.

Are you patient enough to handle the electricity going off three times a day and/or tradespeople not arriving when promised? Can you survive without your favorite brands of consumables? Does it matter that you need to take two flights to get to the nearest international airport? If possible, take an extended holiday to your intended retirement location. Try to live there as you would as an expatriate and think: *Is this something I want to do day in and day out?*

It is also a good idea to try to meet local residents to find potential friends and to find out about local culture. Do some online research and then contact some of the expatriate clubs and associations to find out how you can meet some like-minded people who could offer first-hand advice on their own relocation experiences to the Caribbean.

Other options. If you are not sure about making the big move, remember that there are other options besides retiring abroad permanently. Instead of selling your home and moving overseas, you might consider buying or renting a small home in your destination country and spending only part of the year abroad. This way you may not need to go through the red tape of getting a retirement visa (although you will likely still need a visa of some kind—as well as special approval to invest in the country) and you should not need to sever ties as much with your home country, family and local community back home.

Your retirement dream. Of all the stages in your life, retirement really should be one in which you allow yourself the freedom to think big and live in a location that will make you happy. If you want to retire abroad and you have done your due diligence, then go for it, live out your dream—and enjoy your retirement!

Aging Parents

Q. I have a constant feeling of guilt that my life in France does not seem to have room in it to help care for my aging parents back "home." How can I reconcile this sense of guilt, and what tips can you give me to manage this situation successfully?

A. Caring for aging parents is a complex yet increasingly common responsibility for younger generations. According to the United Nations, by 2050, for the first time in history, the number of elderly around the world is predicted to exceed the number of children. This phenomenon will have widespread effects, including for expatriates working thousands of miles from aging relatives. "Sandwich generation" expats—caring for aging parents while still raising their own children—will feel these effects even more.

Living on the opposite side of the world from aging parents (and other family members) brings with it some unique issues and dynamics that may not arise for families living in the same neighborhood. The biggest and most obvious issue is the coordination of your parents' day-to-day care and support. The second is dealing with your own sense of guilt for being far away when your parents need you. This feeling of guilt can be exacerbated by family members back home, who might feel inequitably burdened by day-to-day caregiving responsibilities and feel the need to make that known. One secret in dealing with both of these issues is clear and timely communication.

Talking with your family. It is a good idea to sit down face-to-face with your family and/or other significant caregivers and determine exactly what your parents want or require in terms of care and support. While you have your family together, discuss possible care requirements for the future as well. Take this time to talk through options with all family members, including your parents if that is possible. Aim to make decisions that are in the best interests of your parents but are also sensitive to the needs and time restraints of each member of your family. Making decisions through consensus will help to avoid bitter arguments in the future that accuse you of not taking the needs of other family members into account.

Talk through who will be the primary caregiver(s) and how other family members will support the primary caregiver(s) and still offer some level of care and support to your parents. The goal is to make some decisions and confirm each family member's commitment. However, decisions may not be reached on day one, so try not to lose your patience or your focus. Just keep working slowly each day to a point where decisions can be made and committed to.

Remember at all times that your conversations should be open and respectful as you gently discuss your parents' wishes, needs and abilities, based on their mental, emotional and physical conditions as well as the wishes of each family member involved in their care.

Enlisting people to help. When talking through the practicalities, remember that you may be able to enlist some help from friendly neighbors or personal friends of your parents. But again, be mindful of their needs and do not overburden your family's allies.

You may also wish to consider engaging professionals. For example, you may need to hire nurses for medical care and elder care advocates to help you or your parents navigate the local medical system. You may also wish to find friendly, reliable and trustworthy "companions" who could take your parents out once a week for a day-trip or perhaps even just to visit the supermarket and their doctor.

If need be, you could also consider hiring a geriatric case manager to take over the hands-on role of coordinating and adjusting each of these local care options as needed.

If your parents genuinely require it, you could consider moving them to a retirement village or nursing home, to ensure they are safe and cared for, plus reduce your own anxieties about their well-being.

Attending to administrative affairs. While you are at home, it is a good idea to complete any privacy and information release permission forms with your parents' medical providers. This will enable you to check in on your parents' health and medical needs and discuss issues of concern with their doctor(s) over the phone, which may help to alleviate some of the guilt you may be experiencing from living far away.

Some families split the responsibility for parents' affairs along practical lines, such as financial, legal, physical support, and so on. This is a great option for expatriate children who want to help their parents but are not geographically close to help with issues like physical support or weekly visits.

Appoint someone in your family to oversee your parents' finances and/or hire a professional to help you take care of this very important task. Be aware though that family money issues can be very sensitive, and emotions can sometimes lead participants to make wrong or impulsive decisions. There is also benefit in starting to build a relationship now with a trusted professional to help where and when needed (and maybe to help your parents avoid turning to an unscrupulous advisor later on).

Communicating with your parents. In terms of communicating easily with your parents: help your parents obtain and use cheap overseas phone cards; have your home and mobile numbers programmed into their phones—and provide them with a small, wallet-sized information card that contains important numbers; perhaps set them up on email and teach them how to use it; and/ or set them up on Skype (or another similar voice-over-Internet protocol or VoIP), which makes calling abroad both easy and affordable.

Make a concerted effort yourself to keep in touch with your parents regularly, both in your preferred manner (which may be phone calls or emails) and in your parents' preferred manner (which may be physical letters and postcards).

Overcoming your guilt. Finally, with regards to your feelings of guilt, ask yourself these questions to see if your guilt is truly worthy of weighing you down each day: Do you not care about your parents and their well-being? Are you not sensitive and responsive to their reasonable needs or requests? Have you been neglectful of your parents? If yes, how exactly? Do you feel you have been rude to them or forgotten their special occasions?

Chances are that apart from not being there physically, you have very little reason to harbor any guilt, so you need to turn this energy into positive support for your parents and a positive outlook on your time spent abroad.

Like anything in life, being as prepared as possible is really your key to reducing both your and your family's anxiety levels with regards to caring for your aging parents. Invest time now in planning for all possible scenarios, make sure you call home often, visit when you can, and follow through on any commitments you have made for parental care.

Then, knowing that you are doing all that you can, let go of any guilt you have and enjoy your time abroad!

Chapter 6

Repatriation

Sudden Exit

Q. Hi. We moved to Sri Lanka three months ago for my husband's job. We finally found a fabulous apartment and moved in our two hundred boxes last weekend. I have defied the odds and got a "proper" job with an American HR consultancy here starting next month. We both love being here, love the shape our life is starting to take, and have been really looking forward to learning and growing from our experiences with the people and culture here.

However, things suddenly took a turn for the worse when my husband came home last week and announced that his company is restructuring and he no longer has a job! I cannot begin to tell you how sad, hurt, angry, frustrated and lost I feel. Unfortunately, I have been taking this anger out on my husband even though I know what has happened is not his fault. This only makes me feel guilty and more annoyed at everything.

I have no idea what we are going to do now. I know we are going to be okay, but any clues as to how to salvage my sanity and be supportive in the interim?

A. Sometimes, just as you start to get settled and, as you say, life takes shape, you have the rug pulled out from underneath you. You probably felt the same way years ago, if anyone ever stole your lunchbox at school. It is that same sense of loss, anger and lack of control. You have every right to be upset and to voice how you feel.

Safely airing your frustrations. It is easy to let negative emotions engulf you after receiving bad news. Take a deep breath and try to assess the situation calmly, rationally and objectively. You and your husband would be wise to take some time to tell each other how angry you are at the situation: detail specific things that annoy you the most about the impending changes (such as the loss of your husband's job and potentially the loss of your job, lack of energy to repack all your boxes and move again, not knowing where you will move to, and more). It is a good idea to do this together for two reasons: one, it helps to validate your feelings if you hear someone else is suffering too; and two, if you hear how the situation impacts your spouse, you are probably less likely to blame him for your losses.

There is a big difference between anger and blame, and the affability of your relationship will depend upon knowing the difference. We suspect your husband will feel slightly if not entirely responsible for the upheaval in your lives, which is why you need to vent your anger at the situation itself and not at your partner. As well as bearing responsibility (financial) and guilt (for relocating you both to Sri Lanka), he may also be nursing a bruised ego for losing his job, and is now facing the dreaded fear of the unknown. Try to think how you would feel in his shoes. Do your best to be supportive, despite your anger at it all.

Survival techniques. Now is a good time for you and your husband to focus on looking after your health and your relationship. It is easy to feel negative and let your circumstances drag you down. However, try to think how you can get your head around what has happened and turn it into something positive. Try not to put your life on hold. How you choose to deal with this "imposition" is something you do have control over; you can choose to wallow in self-pity and stress yourself out, or you can take a step back from the current situation and allow yourselves some time to think "big picture" about your future.

If you are not sure how long you will stay in Sri Lanka, go out and enjoy being a tourist in your city—do some guilt-free sight-seeing, take some day-trips to renowned sites, relax at a few nice coffee shops, or something else that is both positive and makes you feel alive, in control and energized.

Keeping upbeat is difficult when you are playing the waiting game, but do not think you need to do it alone. If you confide in your closest friends and family members (at home and abroad), you might be touched and heartened by how supportive your loved ones can be. It could also be very cathartic to voice your feelings to people who care about you, but who are more removed from the situation than you and your husband.

Another way to get this same sense of "release" from your emotions is to write everything down in a journal and/or in a blog. If you do this every day, each day should get easier than the next, and you can look back on this time as yet another example of your ability to be resilient abroad.

Keeping job connections. In terms of your job offer in Sri Lanka, you might get to start your job if your husband finds out that you will still stay in Sri Lanka for several months more. (Believe it or not, it is not uncommon in company restructures for people to keep their jobs for months if not years after a redundancy announcement.)

But even if you never start that job, it might still be advantageous in two ways. First, you can draw on the confidence boost you received from that job offer, to be optimistic about your future and your ability to get another wonderful job offer elsewhere. Second, if your employing company has an office in your next location, maybe they can hire you there?

Being patient. With time, your options will become clearer, decisions will become more informed, and you will likely become more open to suggestions about what to do next.

So be patient with your future. It has the potential to be magnificent!

Death Abroad

Q. My friend's husband collapsed and died suddenly here at work this week from a brain tumor. It was terrible. Like any best friend would, I have been doing my best to console my friend, offer support in her time of need and help as best as I can with her two young children. But I really feel out of my depth: first with grief counseling and now with helping her to transport his body home from the Czech Republic. I have no idea what I am doing and really need help.

A. First and foremost, our sincere condolences for your friend's loss. This will be a very difficult time for her and she really does need supportive and loving friends like you.

The death of a relative or friend is a true time of crisis. If it happens abroad, the distress can be made worse by the isolation and the numerous practical issues that arise when dealing with death overseas.

In essence, there are two aspects for you to focus on: the emotional side and the practical side.

The emotional side. You may or may not be aware of the grief cycle—a cycle of five emotional states commonly experienced by those facing personal loss and death or dying. Knowledge of the grief cycle is particularly useful in helping to understand and provide support for those suffering. The five stages are denial, anger, bargaining, depression and acceptance. If you have not already, it would be very helpful for you to read up on and familiarize yourself with the stages that your friend will probably experience.

Be aware though that while this is the common cycle, your friend may not experience each and every step, the steps may not necessarily come in the order noted here, and she may even return to one or more stages several times before working through it.

But the important thing is that she does work through these stages, somehow. While your love and support is absolutely necessary, you may want to suggest she also meets with a professional counselor. The old cliché "Time heals all wounds" is most often true, but sometimes, grievers get stuck in one stage of the grieving process and need some extra help to move on. This can especially be the case for expatriates, who due to all the legalities and paperwork, geographical and cultural barriers, plus lack of their usual close support network at home, may not find the time to grieve properly and as a result, may struggle to emotionally reconcile their loss. Ask around some of the expatriate groups and associations in your city to see if they are able to recommend a reputable grief counselor for your friend.

There is also a vast treasure of information and shared experiences online you may want to direct your friend to, and, indeed, check out yourself. Spend some time researching information-based websites, online communities, chat rooms and online support sites for those who are grieving. Find some of the best ones and have them on hand for when your friend is ready to look at them. Do not be offended if she is not ready to receive everything you give her. Just do what you would like someone to do for you, and then remember to put down the research list and still be there for her emotionally.

Your own emotions are also important. Expect to be tired, emotionally exhausted, confused, feeling helpless and sometimes feeling unappreciated. But try to put yourself in your friend's place and respect that she is not in a position to "give" you much in return right now. You will need to draw your strength from other avenues (such as a good night's sleep, a healthy diet, exercise, and the emotional support of your own friends and family).

The practical side. Not being sure exactly which practical step you have reached, we share here some general information for expatriates about the practical aspects of living and dying abroad.

Documentation. As soon as expatriates arrive to live in a new country, they should register with their consulate or embassy. (They might also want to make their residency status official in their home country by informing their tax agency, just so there are no questions if something happens.) Then, should a death in their family occur, their foreign office should be able to advise and assist in registering the death in the country where the person died. They will need to provide documents from themselves and from the person who died which show names, dates of birth and passport details. They will also need to inform the local authorities whether the person suffered from an infectious condition such as hepatitis or HIV, so the authorities are prepared when dealing with the body.

On a morbid but important note, it is worth being aware that in some countries it is possible that a postmortem (autopsy) may be carried out without any express permission from the expatriate or their family, and organs may be removed and kept during this procedure without prior knowledge or consent.

Medical insurance. As an expatriate, it is extremely important to ensure you have good medical insurance coverage and a reputable service provider, because you will be astounded at the costs involved with repatriating a body. In most global packages, repatriation of mortal remains is included, but expatriates should read the fine print. The repatriation of mortal remains typically covers body preparation, paperwork, associated certificates, coffin, and transportation of the body or ashes of the insured from place of death to home country, and then to an agreed funeral home.

More often than not, the insurance company (or the international assistance companies who will act as their intermediaries or facilitators) will be able to assist with much of the paperwork, operating in conjunction with international funeral directors and various governmental bodies. Essential documentation includes a death certificate, embalming certificate, "no objection" certificates from various government ministries, and a "sealing of the coffin" certificate undertaken in the presence of an embassy official from the country receiving the body.

Culture and the law. The cultural and legal aspects of death and dying are as varied across the globe as the practices of marriage and divorce. No two countries are alike, and as morbid as it might seem, it is in every expatriate's best interest to be aware of the cultural and legal practices surrounding death in their current country of residence. Cultural practices and religious laws can come into conflict and seriously complicate the matter of returning mortal remains. The assistance and backing of the likes of your foreign office and international assistance companies can make the process much smoother.

In the absence of a will, different countries, cultures and religions can also significantly impact financial and legal processes. Often bank accounts are frozen and the family is not allowed to (easily) leave the country if no will is in place. This is especially important in areas such as the Middle East where Sharia law presides. Expatriates should consider it their responsibility to themselves and their family to have a legal will drawn up. In the unlikely event that it will be called upon, this document will make a painful and tragic situation a little less stressful.

Emergency preparation. Finally, there is merit in the old adage

"Keep all of your important documents together, as well as cash for emergencies." If you have not already done so, help your friend gather copies of important documents (passports, residency visas, employment contracts, marriage certificates, bank account details, and so on) in one, safe place. Do this for yourself and encourage your other expatriate friends to do so as well. Keep the documents together and somewhere safe where the whole family can locate them quickly if need be.

Your friend will need to access some money fairly readily, so help her get that underway if she does not already have an emergency fund somewhere. If she needs to transfer some money from home, this could take a few days to arrive, so it is best to do this sooner rather than later. If you do not already, you would also be wise to have some money easily accessible, either to fly with your friend to her home, or in the future, to fly to your own home or fly family members to you.

Looking to the future. Your friend will likely need your help for some time, so keep yourself energized and keep up your great supportive efforts. Learn from what your friend is going through and use this tragedy as an opportunity to assess and potentially better structure your own family's affairs.

Our thoughts go out to you, your friend and your families.

Visa Expiry

Q. I am sixty-three, divorced with grown children. I am a teacher by training and two years ago decided that life is too short, so I packed my bags and moved to Africa to teach English to underprivileged children here. I absolutely love what I do and could not feel more valuable or significant in helping these darling children who are so eager to learn. My problem is that now I am at retirement age, the government will not renew my visa and I am not allowed to stay here. I am devastated and heartbroken. What can I do?

A. What a wonderful thing to be teaching underprivileged children in such a fascinating location. We can understand your disappointment and frustration at visa regulations bringing this great experience to an end. Unfortunately it is not until you live abroad that you understand just how significant your passport, visa requirements and the political connections between countries can be.

However, as you are learning, whatever the circumstances and country, it is absolutely imperative that you are at all times aware of all the legal restrictions and requirements pertaining to your host country and your passport citizenship. Be aware too that these may change overnight. It is important to keep abreast of these changes so that you do not find yourself unable to transfer your money out of the country, liable for multiple taxations, or any one of a whole host of other problems.

Renewal options. Regarding your visa, here are several ideas. First, have you spoken to your embassy or consulate about the visa regulations and asked whether there is any way around the current restrictions you are facing? Staff there may be able to suggest a different visa of shorter duration, for example, or be "in the know" about new laws that are forthcoming soon. They may also be willing and/or able to write to the Ministry of Foreign Affairs for a special exemption.

Second, do you have friends who may be able to sponsor you, with a visa from their (or their employer's) company?

Third, if the school is government run, have you checked whether your visa falls under different regulations than the private sector and whether a visa from the latter may extend past the quoted retirement age?

Fourth, in certain countries, things are done somewhat differently, and it might be an idea for you to talk to a *reputable* local immigration agent to see if, in fact, there is another way. Embassies and consulates often keep a list of such immigration agents, so if you do not know whom to approach, try talking to your embassy or consulate.

If all else fails, have you looked into the visa situation in other countries where you might like to extend your teaching adventure? Each country is different with regards to visas and work permits, and it may be that either another African country or somewhere totally different has a more lenient view on age and would grant you a visa. Perhaps your current school could even help connect you to an educational institution elsewhere.

Unplanned repatriation. If staying in your current location is not an option, you may need to cherish the time you spent teaching in Africa and return to your home country... at least until you decide what to do next. This is called an "unplanned repatriation"—very common among military families and, due to the global economic crisis of late, among the families of finance (and other) experts who have been unexpectedly repatriated.

An unplanned repatriation has the potential to be much more emotionally disruptive than a normal repatriation. In addition to the normal challenges associated with returning to your home country, your visa situation may provoke within you an additional sense of loss, as well as feelings of powerlessness, sadness, depression and grief. Reconciliation and grief are an important part of the repatriation process, and it is important that if or when you leave, you take time to say goodbye to people and places properly, plus allow yourself time to grieve once you return home.

Fresh opportunities. When you return home, remember that opportunities and connections with your host country and school do not have to cease. Have you thought about doing something to help them out from home? Could you look into establishing a charitable organization, to financially help the school and its children from a distance?

Could you spend a month or two (depending on the tourist visa situation) at the school conducting a special program, such as organizing a camp, offering an intensive language course or doing something else that the school administrators would like help with?

Could you set up a website to help raise awareness of the area and the school? Could you contribute to other local charities that could restore in you that sense of feeling valuable and significant to the community?

The future. If you think that you will miss the travel opportunities in Africa, remember that a tourist visa should allow you access to most countries in the future, so leaving Africa now does not mean that you can never travel and experience life in Africa again.

If it is the social aspect of working abroad that you will miss, think about connecting online with like-minded individuals who love traveling and perhaps have also taught in Africa. Many a friendship has been made online, enriching both your life and lives around you.

Hopefully, if you leave Africa, you will still take many good memories with you. Focus on these good memories.

Our wish for you is that if you leave, you will go on to find elsewhere the same joy and sense of satisfaction that you found when teaching in Africa.

An Affair Upon Repatriation

Q. My husband and I lived abroad for five and a half years, in Amsterdam, Belgrade and Muscat. We moved home eighteen months ago, but my husband undertook a high-travel role to maintain his senior profile in his company, and consequently he has not been home much since we repatriated. This has definitely put a strain on our relationship, and last month he told me that for the first time in our eleven years together, he cheated on me.

Needless to say, I was, and still am, devastated. We do not have children, so from a practical perspective, I can easily tell him to pack his bags and leave, as I am completely shattered and living the pain of his unfaithfulness every minute of every day. However, I cannot lose our eleven-year love overnight.

If it matters, my husband genuinely seems to be remorseful—he keeps crying about it and has voluntarily gone to see a psychologist twice a week. But my question is, how did this happen? I always thought extramarital affairs happen more in the expat community. So why, after so long abroad, has he had his first affair now? Was it a side effect of so much travel? If so, how can I possibly stand by and agree to his ongoing travel commitments, and how can I ever trust him again?

A. What you are living through is indeed a devastating experience and something not discussed in any repatriation handbook. Sadly, extramarital affairs happen every day to all types of couples around the world, whether they are expatriates, repatriates or neither. We do not condone your husband's actions but take heart in the fact that he has taken himself to see a psychologist. Relationships can be inexplicably painful at times, but you make a good point in that it is difficult to throw away your love overnight—especially when there is a strong possibility that he genuinely reciprocates your love, in spite of his horrendous mistake. It takes courage to walk away from a relationship, but it also takes courage to stay, so we applaud your fortitude as you try to work out a plan for the future.

A catch-22 scenario. You inferred that the physical separation caused by your husband traveling so much these past eighteen months has been a strong contributor to recent problems in your relationship. This seems logical, for it is difficult to feel close and connected with someone who is never there. This goes both ways—both parties feel the distance and the tension that results—and is probably how your previously fracture-free relationship has developed new cracks.

Unfortunately, the catch-22 of international experience tends to be that many repatriates end up in high-travel and/or short-term assignments overseas where their skills are needed, valued and financially rewarded. Be careful: what is good for the company (cost savings, in not needing to pay people as expatriates) is not always good for the family.

Change may mean sacrifice. To answer your question about how you can trust your husband to continue to travel so much and possibly accept an overseas assignment again, maybe you cannot. If after talking to you, talking to his psychologist and thinking things through himself, he agrees that his high-travel role contributed significantly to your current marriage crisis, then it makes sense that he needs to better manage his travel schedule or he needs to stop traveling. Talking on the phone or via email is never the same as having someone at home each night to unwind with and confide in after a busy day.

If your husband agrees to seriously reduce his travel (which is surprisingly possible when a crisis hits, as videoconferencing and/or sending delegates are usually quite viable options) or stop traveling altogether, what then?

The first option could be that he asks to be internally reassigned in his company. The second option is that he might need to consider changing companies. Granted, this could be a painful transition for him, but if the choice is the job or the family, is the decision really that complicated?

If you agree that your husband should change jobs, bear in mind how difficult that might be for him, and how, when you least want to give it, he might need support from you too. This is especially true if he cannot find another job easily and/or if his new job brings home much less income than his current job. Would you be willing to support him in his potential job transition and if necessary, make sacrifices (for example, if a large drop in his salary meant you had to curtail your own spending patterns)?

Addressing relationship issues. Beyond the issues of work and travel, you are likely to be dealing with many other issues as a result of your husband's shocking disclosure, such as trust, faith, hope for the future, and the possibility of recovering the love and relationship you had in the past. These are very real issues, and we suggest that both you and your husband use this life juncture to be as completely honest with each other as possible, about what has been working and what has not been working in your relationship.

If there are additional factors that have made either of you unhappy or have contributed to the change in your relationship, then now is the time to communicate openly, regardless of the pain, and to try to create for yourselves a new and improved blueprint for the future that was even better than what you had in the past.

Looking ahead. You are brave to open up and talk about your situation. We hope that together with your husband, his psychologist and perhaps a psychologist of your own, you can formulate some strategies that help both of you to move forward—as individuals and, potentially, as a couple.

All the very best.

Reverse Culture Shock

Q. We have recently moved back to the U.K. from Mumbai, India. My husband is with a large telecommunications company, and we have been away for almost twelve years. We really enjoyed our time away, but now that the children are approaching high school age, we decided it was time to settle down again in the U.K.

However, we are all finding it really difficult to settle back "home." Both my husband and I were born and raised here, and we worked here for several years before venturing abroad. But it just does not feel like home anymore. For our children, who have holidayed here many times but never lived here, it feels even less like home.

We made the move for the good of the family, but so far, this move has not added any good to our family at all. I understand that returning home can produce "reverse culture shock," but do you have any tips for us?

A. As strange as it seems, the challenge of returning to your passport country can sometimes be more stressful than adjusting to a completely foreign culture abroad. Many returning expatriate families go through the same difficult transition that you are experiencing: some adapt relatively quickly, some take a long time to adapt, and some never adapt—opting instead to turn around and go abroad again!

Dashed expectations. Reverse culture shock is typically experienced when the repatriation process does not follow expectations. For example, if you expected your friends and extended family to go out of their way to look after you (just like they did on your home visits), you are in for a rude awakening. People at home typically assume you know how to fit straight into the community again and that you do not need their help and support anymore. Plus, like you, they juggle busy lives with many competing priorities.

If you lived the typical life of a company-transferred family abroad, you most likely socialized with many expatriates in India, who enjoyed listening to your interesting travel stories and always had their own stories to share. Returning home and finding that the conversation focuses more on the weather, renovating the home, and concerns specific to your local area, can come as quite a shock to repatriating families whose conversation interests typically change after living abroad.

This is compounded when others around you cannot understand your "ignorance" about local issues and they are not interested in hearing about your experiences in places they have neither been to nor have any context for. Such a reception can be especially tough on teenagers, who are extremely self-conscious and already sensitive to peer pressure. Your teenagers might feel left out and at odds with their new environment. These are very real emotions and can make repatriation a real challenge.

The truth is that life in your home country is different, the community and culture are different, and most importantly you are different. To adjust to life in a new culture overseas, your perceptions, habits and maybe even your values had to change. Coming home is no different.

Tips for returning families. Transitioning into your new location, successful adaptation into relearning your culture, and the return of happy, smiling family members may take time. Here are some tips to help (some of which you may have already implemented, but they are still good to share here for families planning their own repatriation).

Prepare in advance. Read about and research your new home well before your move. In fact, treat returning home as if you were taking on a new assignment. Give yourself plenty of time to mentally prepare yourself and your family for the eventuality of moving "home." Talk about it for as long as you can before the actual move, which should give family members a chance to come to terms with leaving and what that means for friendships, familiarity and grieving the things they are going to miss. It is important to allow children (and yourselves) time to reflect on their time spent abroad and to say goodbye properly.

Adjust to the idea. Talk positively about your home country and perhaps watch movies about home, eat foods you would eat at home, and talk about what you are going to do when you get home. Creating an enthusiastic mood about the impending move will frame it in a positive light, making the transition appear like a new adventure in itself.

Grieve. Give everyone in the family the space they need to grieve once they have left. Saying goodbye to anything is difficult, but saying goodbye to a place where you have lived for a long time is even more difficult. Rather than sweeping emotions under the carpet, it is better to grieve now and then adapt better in the long term than to hide emotions now but find them resurfacing in a destructive way in years to come.

Be tourists. Take some time when you land back in your home country to travel around and relearn the idiosyncrasies of the "locals." Have a fun and positive family vacation in your "new home" and allow yourselves to be tourists for a while. Doing this as a family is a safe way for each member of the family to slowly come to terms with and adapt to their new culture and environment. Watch television together, read the local newspapers and magazines, and talk about things you observe and/or feel in your "new" home environment.

Be joiners. Once you have settled in a little, join local sports clubs, newcomers or repatriate groups, hobby groups and more. Some cities now have get-togethers for returning expats and/or international social clubs that welcome repatriates. These are a great place to meet like-minded people who can help ease your assimilation into life back home.

Get away. As a family, plan a holiday abroad together in six months or one year's time—so that everyone in the family can both have something fun to look forward to and can retain their international identity in some way.

Share your feelings. Encourage family members to communicate their feelings and frustrations openly and honestly. Give everyone plenty of opportunities to vent their frustrations and to share their discoveries and challenges along the way. Each family member may deal with the transition period differently; some may appear to fit in immediately while others may struggle for quite some time. Make sure each family member feels supported, loved and cherished. Reassure each family member that their feelings are normal.

Making changes. Longing for a previous life is one thing, but one year on, if you find any of you are still experiencing difficulties adapting, it will be time for a more proactive approach.

✳ How can you inspire your family to "think differently"—to reframe how they are viewing their time back home and to come up with some strategies to improve how they feel?

✳ If your children are not enjoying school, is there another school to which they would be better suited? Have you tried to find other children at school that might have repatriated and therefore might better understand your children's emotions?

✻ If your husband or you are working in a role that makes you unhappy, can (either of) you take a leap of faith and change what you are doing?

✻ Is the physical set up of your home conducive to good memories and togetherness, or is it isolating each family member into their own little world?

✻ Would you all be happier if you went to live abroad again? If yes, why? Where would you go and what would you do?

Challenges back home. Repatriation sounds easy, but it is not. There are challenges and hurdles in the repatriation process, just like there are in the expatriation process.

If any family member is genuinely not coping and perhaps showing signs of depression, consider seeking out the help of a professional counselor. This is by no means a negative reflection on the individual family member and should just be seen as another helping hand in the repatriation process.

We hope that with time, your family adapts well and starts to love living at "home." Or alternatively, if you want to be expatriates again, we hope the universe conspires to extend you another amazing expat adventure abroad!

Conclusion

E xpatriate life can be, and almost always is, an incredibly enriching experience. It can stimulate your senses, tantalize your taste buds and introduce you to a world of wonder you might never have experienced had you not dared to pack up your belongings, journey outside your comfort zone, and immerse yourself in the culture of a foreign land.

If you are on a work assignment abroad, your expat years can be a chance to prove that you have what it takes to do well as a career woman in any location. If, on the other hand, you are arriving without the promise of employment, be patient with yourself. Try to reconcile any feelings of loss you might be experiencing from leaving friends, family, social networks and/or a satisfying career back home. Then cherish your newfound blank canvas. Revitalize your inner spirit, spend more time with your children, lend much-needed volunteer support to local charity organizations, pursue your passions, or reinvent yourself and your career. Get excited and create an outstanding new life for yourself!

Not every day will be a good day. There will be times when you will question your decisions and feel lost, frustrated, overwhelmed, angry and out of control. But as we have endeavored to illustrate in our collection of answers to real-life confessions, your feelings are completely normal and you are not alone. When you need help, there are people available to help you. Reach out to your new friends, local expat groups, like-minded people online, your partner (if applicable), life coaches, professional counselors, your (or your partner's) employer, and more.

You are a strong woman, capable of overcoming many challenges. Do your best to stay positive, because while many factors influence your happiness abroad, ultimately you are the greatest determinant of your own success.

Thank you again for supporting this book. We hope it has reassured and inspired you on your expatriate journey. The expat rollercoaster can be a fantastic experience, and we wish you an exhilarating ride.

Acknowledgments

This book would not have been possible without the audience of ExpatWomen.com, whose popularization of our Expat Confessions columns inspired the three-year development and refinement of this manuscript. We thank our readers for confirming the genuine need out there for a book about real-life expat concerns and for showing us, by their clicks, which confessions were of the most interest.

We owe a huge debt of gratitude to April Davidson, for allowing us to share her story. Her adjustment abroad served as an ongoing inspiration during our writing process, reminding us that many women might benefit from some reassurance that they are not alone when they are feeling lost or isolated abroad.

Heartfelt thanks go to our key mentor on this project, the renowned repatriate Canadian author and international speaker Robin Pascoe of ExpatExpert.com. We are grateful to Robin for unselfishly sharing her hard-earned publishing wisdom, for continually checking up on our progress and for generously writing this book's foreword.

We thank the equally impressive Jo Parfitt—a British expatriate in the Netherlands who is the author of twenty-eight books and a speaker, publisher and writers' mentor—for being a great friend, mentor and role model in our publishing journey.

A big thank-you to Jeanine Souren, for volunteering her time and expertise to help write the original website versions of some of our early confessions. Jeanine is a registered psychologist in the Netherlands who runs www.ReflectToAct.com, a coaching and psychotherapy business specializing in expatriate issues and consulting mostly via telephone, email, Skype and videoconferencing. Jeanine is a Dutch repatriate who lived with her American husband in India, Canada, Indonesia, Chile and Thailand.

A special thank-you also to Jill Lengré, co-founder of ExpatWomen. com, for her feedback on our early Expat Confessions online. Jill's website input (2006—2007) and her belief in the potential of the Expat Women website helped shape it into the valuable resource it is today.

Warmest thanks to our wonderful copyeditor Naomi Pauls, our eagle-eye proofreader Ashley Thompson, our fabulous cover designer Beth Nori, our talented interior designer Melissa Gerber and our hardworking web designer María Inés Castro Mondragón. They are all brilliant and we cannot thank them enough for their support.

Finally, we would like to thank our friends and families for their love, support and constructive feedback on this book. We especially thank our husbands, Paul and Joe, for taking care of our angels (Bailey and Jasmine, and Grace and Zara) when we needed to sacrifice "family time" to finish everything necessary for this book. We love you all and say a huge thank-you!

About the Authors

 **Andrea Martins** is an Australian who has lived in Brisbane, Melbourne, Canberra, and near the beautiful beaches of the Sunshine Coast. Her experience as an expatriate comes from three years in Jakarta, Indonesia; four years in Mexico City, Mexico; and now nearly two years in Kuala Lumpur, Malaysia, with her French-born Portuguese-Australian husband and two children.

Since ExpatWomen.com's inception in March 2006, Andrea has dedicated her work life to building Expat Women into the treasure chest of information and inspiration that it is today for so many women around the world. She has networked with and learned from countless peers and mentors in the global mobility industry, and she has answered thousands of emails from members, website visitors, peers and clients about a whole range of issues related to living abroad.

Representing ExpatWomen.com, Andrea has been a guest presenter to internationally minded audiences in Houston, Washington, Mexico City, Amsterdam, the Hague, Singapore, Kuala Lumpur, Brisbane, Sydney, Melbourne and Marrakech.

Andrea's professional background includes coordinating large networks in two major government organizations in Australia; working in the Australian embassy in Jakarta; and working as an executive headhunter in an international HR consulting firm in Jakarta. Andrea has a bachelor of arts from the University of Queensland, Australia, and a postgraduate diploma in electronic commerce from La Trobe University, Australia.

Victoria Hepworth is a New Zealander who left in 1996 and has since lived (and worked) in Miyazaki, Japan; Shanghai, China; Saint Petersburg, Russia; Gothenburg, Sweden; and Mumbai, India. Victoria currently lives in Dubai, United Arab Emirates, with her English husband and two young children—the youngest of which was born on the day this manuscript was submitted to our editor!

In 2004, Victoria built on her experience working with expatriate support issues at the private, corporate and nonprofit level to found and help establish Lifeline Shanghai, a not-for-profit telephone hotline for the expatriate community. This gave her enormous insight into the everyday struggles and challenges expats were facing and inspired her to complete her master's degree in psychology. Victoria majored in cross-cultural issues and completed her thesis on the "trailing spouse." She left Shanghai to follow her heart and suddenly found herself living the challenges many of the callers faced, as a new trailing spouse.

From early 2007 to late 2009, Victoria volunteered her time to help write most of the web versions of these confessions. She later went on to work with ExpatWomen.com in an official capacity—answering confessions, assisting with key projects and managing the Expat Women Blog Directory.

Victoria has a bachelor of business in human resources and a master of arts in psychology, both from Massey University, New Zealand. She also has a diploma in clinical nutrition from Stonebridge Associated Colleges in the United Kingdom.

About ExpatWomen.com

ExpatWomen.com was created by two friends, Australian Andrea Martins and American Jill Lengré, when they were both living as expatriates in Mexico City. Andrea and Jill worked together on the website for two years (one year prior to launch in January 2007 and one year after launch) before Jill stepped aside to focus on her move back to the United States. Andrea now runs the website as an expatriate in Kuala Lumpur, Malaysia, and Jill now lives and works as a senior product manager for an information technology company in California.

ExpatWomen.com is the largest global website helping women living abroad. Its mission is to "inspire your success abroad." To this end, it displays more than 1,000 quality content pages, 1,600+ expat women blogs, 300+ readers' stories, individual country resource pages, interviews with successful expat women, loads of motivational articles, and an inspirational blog and monthly newsletter.

Thanks to the valued support of its members, mentors, sponsors, advertisers, editorial contributors and peer networks, Expat Women.com currently receives more than 30,000 unique visitors per month and has 10,000+ members, from 165+ nationalities, based in 187+ countries.

ExpatWomen.com Testimonials

"I am blown away by your website..."

—*Juliana Carrozzi, an American in Nicaragua, November 2008*

"I absolutely love, love, love the expat women website. It has been a real life saver."

—*Rupal Dalal, an American in Mexico City, May 2007*

"Just wanted to let you know I think your website is simply amazing, such a wealth of resources, and such interesting people... absolutely super, the best on the net..."

—*Mary van der Boon, a Canadian in the Netherlands, October 2009*

"ExpatWomen.com keeps me sane on bad days! The last few months have been very challenging albeit I would do it all again in a heartbeat... your website is amazing... Keep doing what you're doing... it's just wonderful!"

—*Judy Herde, a New Zealander in China, January 2010*

"I am so impressed with your site for expat women! I wish this had been around 15 years ago when I started my journey!"

—*Elizabeth Kruempelmann, an American in Germany, June 2008*

"Keep up the good work, really, people like me are so grateful you are there."

—*Alex Taylor, a Brit in the United States, January 2010*

"You have made a wonderful difference in my life."

—*Karen Van Drie, an American in the Czech Republic, January 2010*

"I am sure you get thousands of emails like this, but just wanted to be among the very many who want to say thank you! You've lifted my spirit to such [a] high point that 'thank you' seems way too inadequate!"

—*Bahareh Abghari, an Iranian in the United States, August 2007*

"I must say, your site is addictive. I have recently started a business, serving expatriates living overseas, and have gleaned a tremendous amount of useful information and contacts from your site. You have done a fabulous job highlighting the creative talents and skills of an interesting group of women."

—*Susan Bernstein, an American repatriate, October 2010*

"I have to congratulate you on your site! It's a brilliant idea and quite the lifesaver! It's incredibly comforting to know one is not alone!"

—*Diana Carolina, a Mexican in Colombia, December 2008*

"It's such a pleasure to read all the stories: it motivates and helps me to go further with my own ideas and opportunities."

—*Monika Khaled, an Austrian in Singapore, January 2011*

"I have to tell you what I'm seeing so far is unbelievable. I have been living on an island for four years now. I decided to put this to prayer, and then my friend sent me your link this morning. This is an awesome idea!"

—*Jeannette Smith, an American, April 2007*

Resources

Books

Ashman, Anastasia M., & Eaton Gökmen, Jennifer (Editors). 2006. *Tales from the Expat Harem: Foreign Women in Modern Turkey.* Seal Press.

Brayer Hess, Melissa, & Linderman, Patricia. 2007. *The Expert Expat: Your Guide to Successful Relocation Abroad.* Revised edition. Nicholas Brealey Publishing.

Bruce, Lindy. 2008. *Motherhood and Me: Learn to Embrace What Is Wonderful about Motherhood and Gracefully Survive the Rest.* MouseHand.

Bryson, Debra R., & Hoge, Charise M. 2005. *A Portable Identity: A Woman's Guide to Maintaining a Sense of Self while Moving Overseas.* Revised edition. Transition Press International.

Burnett, Mark. 2006. *Jump In! Even If You Don't Know How to Swim.* Ballantine Books.

Copeland, Anne P. 2004. *Global Baby.* The Interchange Institute.

Eldridge, Sherrie. 1999. *Twenty Things Adopted Kids Wish Their Adoptive Parents Knew.* Delta.

————. 2009. *Twenty Things Adoptive Parents Need to Succeed.* Delta.

Ferriss, Timothy. 2009. *The 4-Hour Workweek: Escape 9–5, Live Anywhere, and Join the New Rich.* 2nd edition. Crown Archetype.

Frost, Maya. 2009. *The New Global Student: Skip the SAT, Save Thousands on Tuition and Get a Truly International Education.* Three Rivers Press.

Global Connection B.V. 2009. *Expat and Travel Stories: Volume 1.* Global Connection B.V.

————. 2009. *Repats: From Expat to Repat: The Last Turn in the Rollercoaster.* Global Connection B.V.

———— (Editor). 2010. *Expat & Partner Guide.* Global Connection B.V.

Goodman, Michelle. 2008. *My So-Called Freelance Life: How to Survive and Thrive as a Creative Professional for Hire.* Seal Press.

Grady Huskey, Joanne. 2009. *The Unofficial Diplomat: A Memoir.* New Academia Publishing/SCARITH Books.

Gray, Vicky. 2009. *Didgeridoos and Didgeridon'ts: A Brit's Guide to Moving Your Life Down Under.* Lean Marketing Press.

Gregory, Joe, & Jenkins, Debbie. 2009. *The Wealthy Author: The Fast Profit Method for Writing, Publishing and Selling Your Non-fiction Book.* Publishing Academy.

Guzmán, Alejandra, Kuguru, Ruth, & Rochester, Lisa Blunt. 2010. *Thrive: Thirty-four Women. Eighteen Countries. One Goal.* Shanghai, China edition. Grace Publishing Company.

Heinzer, Jeanne A. 2009. *Living Your Best Life Abroad: Resources, Tips and Tools for Women Accompanying Their Partners on an International Move.* Summertime Publishing.

Henry De Tessan, Christina (Editor). 2002. *Expat: Women's True Tales of Life Abroad.* Seal Press.

Holland, Angus, & Ross, Emily. 2005. *100 Great Businesses and the Minds Behind Them.* Random House Australia.

————. 2007. *50 Great e-Businesses and the Minds Behind Them.* Random House Australia.

Hughes, Katherine L. 1998. *The Accidental Diplomat: Dilemmas of the Trailing Spouse.* Aletheia Publications.

Kamata, Suzanne (Editor). 2009. *Call Me Okaasan: Adventures in Multicultural Mothering.* Wyatt-MacKenzie Publishing.

Keenan, Brigid. 2005. *Diplomatic Baggage: The Adventures of a Trailing Spouse.* John Murray.

Kilborn, Peter T. 2009. *Next Stop, Reloville: Life Inside America's New Rootless Professional Class.* Times Books.

Knorr, Rosanne. 2008. *The Grown-Up's Guide to Running Away from Home.* 2nd edition. Ten Speed Press.

Kruempelmann, Elizabeth. 2004. *The Global Citizen: A Guide to Creating an International Life and Career.* Ten Speed Press.

_____. 2010. *The Global Citizen's Get Started Guide to Working Abroad: For Students, Professionals and Expats.* Global Citizen Press.

Kunst, My-Linh, & Zabusky, Charlotte Fox. 2008. *Beyond Borders: Portraits of American Women from Around the World.* My-Linh Kunst.

Monosoff, Tamara. 2010. *Your Million Dollar Dream: Regain Control and Be Your Own Boss. Create a Winning Business Plan. Turn Your Passion into Profit.* McGraw-Hill.

Nevadomski Berdan, Stacie. 2011. *Go Global! A Student's Guide to Launching an International Career.* EKR Media.

_____, & Yeatman, Perry C. 2007. *Get Ahead by Going Abroad: A Woman's Guide to Fast-Track Career Success.* William Morrow.

Olofsson, Gwyneth. 2004. *When in Rome, or Rio, or Riyadh... Cultural Q&As for Successful Business Behavior around the World.* Intercultural Press.

Parfitt, Jo. 2006. *Expat Entrepreneur: How to Create and Maintain Your Own Portable Career Anywhere in the World.* Lean Marketing Press.

_____. 2008. *A Career in Your Suitcase.* 3rd edition. Lean Marketing Press.

_____. 2009. *Release the Book Within.* 2nd edition. Bookshaker.com.

_____. 2010. *Write Your Life Stories: Learn How to Add Spice to Your Life Stories.* Summertime Publishing.

Pascoe, Robin. 2000. *Homeward Bound: A Spouse's Guide to Repatriation.* Expatriate Press.

_____. 2003. *A Moveable Marriage: Relocate Your Relationship Without Breaking It.* Expatriate Press.

_____. 2006. *Raising Global Nomads: Parenting Abroad In An On-Demand World.* Expatriate Press.

_____. 2009. *A Broad Abroad: The Expat Wife's Guide to Successful Living Abroad.* Expatriate Press.

Patterson, Jennifer A. C. 2006. *When Families Cross Borders: A Guide for Internationally Mobile People.* Cross Border Publishing.

Pollock, David C., & Van Reken, Ruth E. 2009. *Third Culture Kids: Growing Up Among Worlds.* Revised edition. Nicholas Brealey Publishing.

Quick, Tina L. 2010. *The Global Nomad's Guide to University Transition.* Summertime Publishing.

Reuvid, Jonathan. 2010. *Working Abroad: The Complete Guide to Overseas Employment and Living in a New Country.* 31st edition. Kogan Page.

Sabet Tavangar, Homa. 2009. *Growing Up Global: Raising Children to Be at Home in the World.* Ballantine Books.

Summers Hargis, Toni. 2006. *Rules, Brittania: An Insider's Guide to Life in the United Kingdom.* Thomas Dunne Books.

Weston, Marian. 2007. *Alone at Home: The Practical Guide for Those Coping Alone.* Swift Transitions.

Zurer Pearson, Barbara. 2008. *Raising a Bilingual Child: A Step-by-Step Guide for Parents.* Living Language.

Websites

The Adoption Guide
www.theadoptionguide.com/process
Adoption help and advice from a leading American adoption magazine.

Adoptive Families
www.adoptivefamilies.com/transracial-adoption.php
Advice for families before, during and after adoption, from an award-winning American adoption magazine.

Advance
www.advance.org
A global community for Australians living abroad.

Aetna Global Benefits
www.goodhealthworldwide.com/Aetna
A leading global provider of healthcare to expatriates.

Aging Care
www.agingcare.com
Resources, support and information to help deal with the stress of aging parents and elder care.

Aging Parents and Elder Care
www.aging-parents-and-elder-care.com
Information, resources and support for navigating elder care.

Al-Anon/Alateen
www.al-anon.alateen.org
Information about alcoholism and support and recovery programs in English, Spanish and French.

Alcoholics Anonymous
www.aa.org
The official site for worldwide Alcoholic Anonymous (AA) services.

Allied
www.allied.com
A well-known global relocation company. For domestic and international moves.

Allo' Expat Home
www.alloexpat.com
Country-specific information and community forums for over one hundred locations.

American Domestic Violence Crisis Line
www.866uswomen.org
Founded by repatriate Paula Lucas, who tells an inspiring personal story of escape from domestic violence abroad. The organization provides information about domestic violence, with a hotline number for American expats. The U.S. hotline number (866) 879-6636 (866-USWOMEN) is toll free, so victims can contact the Crisis Line directly from anywhere, at any time. *(Warning: Please remember that your emails and website searches can be tracked from your computer. If you fear for your safety, you might prefer to use a computer other than your own to visit sites like this one.)*

Anglo Info
www.angloinfo.com
A local business directory for English-speaking expats in various countries.

Antiques Diva
www.antiquesdiva.com
A wonderful example of an expat woman reinventing herself abroad with a creative business built on her passion. Well done, Toma Haines.

Associates of the American Foreign Service Worldwide
www.aafsw.org
A nonprofit organization representing U.S. Foreign Service spouses, employees and retirees since 1960.

Barclays Wealth International
www.expat.barclays.com/expatriate
Banking, investment and wealth management services designed for expatriates.

Bloomberg
www.bloomberg.com
Business news from around the world.

BPW International
www.bpw-international.org
The International Federation of Business and Professional Women was started in 1930. It has affiliate clubs all around the world, which strive to develop the leadership potential of women.

BR Anchor Publishing
www.branchor.com
Publishes books that prepare individuals and families for domestic and international relocation.

British Expat
www.britishexpat.com
News, humor and information for Brits worldwide.

British Expats
www.britishexpats.com
A resource for British expats, including information about living and relocating overseas and general discussion forums.

Career By Choice
www.careerbychoiceblog.com
A great blog by expat career and personal branding coach Megan Fitzgerald, with success tips for expatriates interested in building a career or business that fits their international lifestyle.

Career Resource Center for Expatriates (CRCE)
www.aasingapore.com/crce
Offers information and training sessions for expatriates seeking job opportunities in Singapore.

Clements International
www.clements.com
Since 1947, Clements International has been providing innovative insurance solutions to individuals and organizations operating outside of their home country.

Co-Parenting
www.coparenting101.org
A site dedicated to helping divorced couples co-parent when their marriage ends.

Crave
www.thecravecompany.com
Publishes inspiring books that feature women entrepreneurs in various cities in the U.S. and abroad.

Cross Border Planning
www.crossborderplanning.com
Provides cross-border financial planning advice.

Cross Cultural Kid
www.crossculturalkid.org
Website of Ruth Van Reken—author, international speaker and expert on third culture and cross-cultural kids.

Culture Crossing
www.culturecrossing.net
A community-built guide to cross-cultural etiquette and understanding.

Divorced Women Online
www.divorcedwomenonline.com
Information, resources and support for divorced women.

Domestic Violence
www.domesticviolence.org
Information on domestic violence, with personal safety plans.

E Diplomat
www.ediplomat.com
Reports on diplomatic living conditions in posts around the world.

Easy Expat
www.easyexpat.com
Provides expatriates with information about living abroad.

Elance
www.elance.com
A great site to both find and outsource freelance work.

Escape Artist
www.escapeartist.com
A website about living overseas, retiring abroad, international real estate, and asset protection.

European Professional Women's Network (EPWN)
www.europeanpwn.net
Coordinates local networking groups, which support the career progress of women.

European Relocation Association (EuRA)
www.eura-relocation.com
A well-known industry body for relocation professionals—both in Europe and worldwide. Founded in 1998.

Expat Arrivals
www.expatarrivals.com
Includes information and expat resources for many locations.

Expat Blog
www.expat-blog.com
A comprehensive expatriate blog directory.

The Expat Coach Directory
www.theexpatcoachdirectory.com
Lists expat coaches to help you transition, and live, successfully in your new country.

Expat Exchange
www.expatexchange.com
Information about international living and the expatriate life.

Expat Expert
www.expatexpert.com
Robin Pascoe's website, designed to assist expatriate families living and working overseas—and returning home.

Expat Finder
www.expatfinder.com
A global search engine for expat-related services.

Expat Focus
www.expatfocus.com
A global relocation advice site for expatriates.

Expat Forum
www.expatforum.com
Hosts networking forums for expatriates.

Expat Forums
www.expatforums.org
Another site hosting networking forums for expatriates.

Expat Info Desk
www.expatinfodesk.com
Provides relocation information and also offers digital books about popular expat destinations.

Expat Interviews
www.expatinterviews.com
A website that interviews expats about living and working abroad.

Expat KL
www.expatkl.com
This company runs various useful online sites and also publishes a great monthly magazine for expatriates living in Malaysia.

Expat Money Channel
www.expatmoneychannel.com
A financial website with information dedicated to British expatriates living abroad.

Expat Network
www.expatnetwork.com
An expat portal with community, career, contract and financial information.

Expatica
www.expatica.com
News and information for the international community.

Expatriate Archive Centre
www.xpatarchive.com
Collects, preserves, promotes and makes accessible a collection of primary source materials, documenting the global social history of expatriate life.

Expatriate Healthcare
www.expatriatehealthcare.com
They provide medical insurance coverage for expatriates living and working abroad.

Expats Radio
www.expatsradio.com
Audio information and entertainment for expatriates worldwide.

Expat Woman
www.expatwoman.com
Primarily for expatriate women in the United Arab Emirates.

Expat Women
www.expatwomen.com
The largest global website helping women living abroad. The website displays over 1,000 quality content pages, expat club and international school listings for around 200 countries, 300+ readers' stories, expat women blogs, interviews with successful expatriate women, loads of motivational articles, and an inspirational blog and monthly newsletter.

Expat Women Blog Directory
www.expatwomen.com/expatblog
Part of the ExpatWomen.com site, this blog directory features 1,600+ expat women blogs from all over the world and is a great resource for networking with other women abroad.

Explorer Publishing
www.explorerpublishing.com
Publishes fabulous location-specific guides for living and working in various locations.

Families in Global Transition
www.figt.org
Hosts an annual conference to bring together a wide range of providers and professionals who support families living abroad.

Family Liaison Office (FLO)
www.state.gov/m/dghr/flo
Part of the U.S. Department of State, the FLO office services U.S. government direct-hire employees, their family members and Members of Household (MOH) who are serving, have served or will serve abroad.

Federation of American Women's Clubs Overseas (FAWCO)
www.fawco.org
A network of independent, American and international volunteer organizations representing Americans living abroad.

Firefly Coaching
www.fireflycoaching.com
The website for expat Stephanie Ward, who runs a wonderful marketing coaching service for entrepreneurs.

First Wives World
www.firstwivesworld.com
Resources and a community network for women coping with divorce.

Focus
www.focus-info.org
Services and resources for Internationals in the UK. Founded in 1982.

Foreign Service Youth Foundation
www.fsyf.org
Supports children, teens and families affiliated with U.S. foreign affairs agencies.

The Forum for Expatriate Management (FEM)
www.totallyexpat.com
Provides a news and information portal for those working in the global mobility arena.

General Foundation of Women's Clubs (GFWC)
www.gfwc.org
One of the world's largest and oldest nonpartisan, nondenominational women's volunteer service organizations. Founded in 1890. More than 100,000 members in affiliated clubs worldwide.

Global Connection
www.global-connection.info
An internationally operating media company, focusing especially on expats and their partners.

Global Nomads Group (GNG)
www.gng.org
An international NGO that creates interactive educational programs for students about global issues. Established in 1998.

Globe Women
www.globewomen.org
Organizes an annual conference for women—in a different part of the world each year.

Going Global
www.goinglobal.com
Provides country-specific career and employment information, including worldwide internship and job postings.

Good Schools Guide International
www.gsgi.co.uk/site
A guide to international schools around the world.

Healing Club
www.healingclub.com
An online support community for domestic violence victims, survivors, or those who know someone who has been affected by domestic violence.

Infidelity
www.infidelity.com
Resources and information for coping with infidelity.

Infidelity Support
www.infidelitysupport.com
Community forum, blog, news and resources for surviving infidelity.

Interaction International
www.interactionintl.org
Co-founded by Dr David C. Pollock, this organization is a voice for third culture kids.

Intercultural Communication Institute (ICI)
www.intercultural.org
A nonprofit organization designed to foster an awareness and appreciation of cultural differences in both the international and domestic arenas.

InterExpat
www.interexpat.com
A global site for news, classifieds, blog listings and expat experiences.

International Adoption Help
www.internationaladoptionhelp.com
Information and resources for American families planning to adopt.

The International Alliance for Women (TIAW)
www.tiaw.org
A non-profit that runs support programs and international conferences for women.

International Inventory of Domestic Violence Services
www.hotpeachpages.net/a/countries.html
A list of domestic violence help agencies in nearly two hundred countries.

International Living
www.internationalliving.com
Information and advice about traveling, retiring, living, buying real estate, investing, and starting a business overseas.

International Therapist Directory
www.internationaltherapistdirectory.com
Online global listing of professional mental health therapists who are familiar with the TCK and international expatriate experiences.

InterNations
www.internations.org
An online and offline community, for expatriates and "global minds."

Jo Parfitt
www.joparfitt.com
Long-term expat and author of many books, Jo is a publisher and writer's mentor who has excellent books and advice about expat life.

Journey Woman
www.journeywoman.com
An online travel resource just for women.

LifeLine Shanghai
www.lifelineshanghai.com
A free, confidential and anonymous helpline for those in Shanghai, China. This is the telephone hotline that our book's co-author, Victoria Hepworth, founded and helped to establish in 2004.

Living Abroad
www.livingabroad.com
In partnership with businesses, provides preparation information, resources and tools for expatriates and their families, international short-term assignees and business travelers.

Lois Freeke
www.loisfreeke.com
An expat career and personal branding strategist.

The McGraw-Hill Companies
www.mcgraw-hill.com
A global publishing, financial, information and media services company.

The Modern Woman's Divorce Guide
www.themodernwomansdivorceguide.com
Written by lawyers and doctors for women in the United States and beyond.

Multilingual Living Magazine
www.multilingualliving.com
A popular digital publication dedicated to families raising bilingual and multilingual children.

Net Expat
www.netexpat.com
A company that addresses the assessment, training and coaching needs of global employees.

Newcomers Club
www.newcomersclub.com
The Newcomers, Moms, Dads & Womens Club Worldwide Directory lists clubs and organizations worldwide that give people new to an area the opportunity to meet.

Newcomers Network
www.newcomersnetwork.com
Friendly, welcoming network in Australia and the UK, run by Sue Ellson.

Now Health International
www.now-health.com
A major new healthcare provider, with a fresh approach to international healthcare.

Outpost Expatriate Support Network
www.outpostexpat.nl
A network of offices around the world that support expatriate families of Shell International B.V.

Paguro
www.paguro.net
An information and networking site for expatriates.

Passport Career
www.passportcareer.com
A dynamic, global job-search tool for organizations to support accompanying partners of international assignees.

Permits Foundation
www.permitsfoundation.com
An international, nonprofit, corporate initiative to promote access for accompanying spouses and partners of international staff to employment, through an improvement of work permit regulations.

A Portable Identity
www.aportableidentity.com
A book and a website, for women who are the trailing spouse in an international relocation.

Reflect to Act
www.reflecttoact.com
A coaching and psychotherapy business that specializes in expatriate issues. Run by repatriate and registered psychologist Jeanine Souren.

Relate
www.relate.org.uk
Relate offers advice, relationship counseling, sex therapy, workshops, mediation, consultations and support face-to-face, by phone and through their website.

Retire Abroad
www.retire-abroad.org
An online magazine for overseas living and retirement.

Ricklin-Echikson Associates (REA)
www.r-e-a.com
A company that provides global transition assistance and career management services to corporations and their individuals.

RNG International Educational Consultants
www.rebeccagrappo.com
A personal, educational consultancy focusing on the needs of expatriate families.

Sally White & Associates
www.sallywhite.com
Specializes in global career management and relocation support services.

School Choice International
www.schoolchoiceintl.com
A leading global education consulting firm for school placement and more.

Shelter Offshore
www.shelteroffshore.com
Resources and information for living abroad.

SIRVA Relocation
www.sirva.com
A leading provider of relocation services in over 130 countries, SIRVA Relocation has been redefining the industry with comprehensive, hassle-free relocation services focused on customers' diverse needs.

Spouse Career Centre
www.spousecareercentre.com
Provides career-related counseling, networking and coaching services to accompanying spouses.

Stacie Berdan
www.stacieberdan.com
Site of Stacie Nevadomski Berdan—international careers expert and author.

Surviving Infidelity
www.survivinginfidelity.com
A community forum for those dealing with a partner's infidelity.

Tales from a Small Planet
www.talesmag.com
A nonprofit site sharing a wealth of stories and information about expatriate life.

TCK World
www.tckworld.com
The official website for Dr. Ruth Hill Useem, who first coined the term "Third Culture Kid."

Teen Suicide Talk
www.teensuicidetalk.com
Help for teens (and their parents) fighting depression and thoughts of suicide.

The Telegraph
www.telegraph.co.uk/expat
News, features and advice for expatriates.

The Telegraph—Blog of Apple Gidley
www.my.telegraph.co.uk/applegidley
Apple Gidley has moved countries many, many times—first as a third culture kid (TCK), and then as an adult with her own third culture kids. She has many wise insights to share.

Third Culture Kids
www.tckworld.com
Resources, tips and information for third culture kids (TCKs).

Trafimar Relocation Services
www.trafimarrelo.com.mx
The leading provider of relocation services in and out of Mexico.

The Trailing Spouse
www.thetrailingspouse.com
The website of Yvonne McNulty, PhD, who is known for her Trailing Spouse survey and her follow-on research on expat return on investment (ROI). Copies of Yvonne's 80-page survey, containing findings from her four-year study of accompanying spouse issues on international assignments, are available for purchase from her website.

Transition Dynamics
www.transition-dynamics.com
A consultancy serving the international expatriate, and repatriate, community. Run by Barbara F. Schaetti, who has given many years of service to FIGT conferences.

Transitions Abroad
www.transitionsabroad.com
Dedicated to work, study, living, and cultural immersion travel abroad since 1977.

U.S. Global Mail
www.usglobalmail.com
Serving expats for the last 15+ years, US Global mail offers mail forwarding and fulfilment services to individuals and corporates.

Women Against Violence in Europe (WAVE)
www.wave-network.org
On their Violence Against Women Directory, you can find contacts of over 4,000 women's help organizations in 46 countries of Europe.

Women's Aid (UK)
www.divorcedwomenonline.com
Information and resources about domestic violence.

Women's International Networking (WIN)
www.winconference.net
Hosts an excellent annual global leadership conference for women.

Worldwide ERC®
www.worldwideerc.org
A well-known workforce mobility association for professionals who oversee, manage or support U.S. domestic and international employee transfer. Founded in 1964.

Yellow Ribbon Suicide Prevention Program
www.yellowribbon.org
A community-based program that offers support and education about suicide and prevention.